Glasgow Curiosities

Glasgow Curiosities

CAROL FOREMAN

JOHN DONALD PUBLISHERS LTD
EDINBURGH

ISBN 0 85976 485 0

British Library Cataloguing in Publication Data.

A catalogue record for this book is available
from the British Library.

Typesetting & origination by Brinnoven, Livingston.
Printed & bound in Great Britain by Bell & Bain Ltd, Glasgow.

CONTENTS

Acknowledgements v

1. The Bird, The Tree, The Fish and The Bell 1

2. Glasgow's Shameful Hidden Past 6

3. The Curse of Bob Dragon, The Ugliest Man in Glasgow 13

4. Joseph Lister: The Glasgow Connection 18

5. Wallace the Fire Dog 27

6. Beau-Idéal of a Glasgow Merchant 31

7. The Balloon Man 39

8. Excursion Train Crashes at St Enoch Station 42

9. The Summer-House on a Raft: The Clyde Freak Ship Livadia 50

10. Thirteen Dead in Glasgow Fire 56

11. The Only Man in Glasgow Who Could Prove He was Sane 62

12. The is no Tea Like Cranston's 70

13. The Barrows Queen 77

14. A Man Ahead of His Time 85

15. West of Scotland Cricket Club, Partick 89

16 Glasgow's Own Doge's Palace 93

17. Some Wee Stories from the Archives   99

18. The Statue with the Moving Tail   104

19. The Clyde's Worst Disaster   108

20. Glasgow Says Farewell to the Leeries   116

21. Police Inspector Shot Dead in High Street   119

22. Riot in the Coliseum Theatre   124

23. A.E. Pickard Unlimited   127

24. Black Days in Soccer History   138

'So You Know Glasgow?' — A Hundred Questions   144

A Hundred Answers   148

– 1 –
THE BIRD, THE TREE, THE FISH
AND THE BELL

The mysterious emblems of Glasgow's patron saint, Mungo or Kentigern, adorning the city's coat-of-arms puzzle both visitors and locals, as does the old rhyme relating to them. No-one understands what it means and the only feasible explanation that anyone has ever come up with is that it aimed to emphasise the legendary nature of the stories surrounding the 6th-century St Mungo brought up in Culross by St Serf.

This is the bird that never flew
This is the tree that never grew
This is the fish that never swam
This is the bell that never rang.

The *Bird*, so the story goes, commemorates St Serf's tame robin, accidentally killed by some of his young disciples who, being envious of Mungo, their master's favourite, hoped to get him into trouble by blaming him. Mungo took the dead bird in his hands and prayed over it. Restored to life it flew chirping to its master.

The *Tree*, an oak, began its legendary life as a few hazel twigs. As a boy in the monastery Mungo fell asleep while left in charge of the holy fire in the refectory. Again, trying to get Mungo into trouble, his companions put out the fire. However, when Mungo awoke and saw what had happened he relit it by breaking off some frozen twigs from a hazel tree and causing them to burst into flame by praying over them.

The *Fish* with a ring in its mouth is a salmon and it tells a story of adultery. Hydderch Hael, King of Cadzow, gave his queen, Languoreth, a ring which she passed on to a courtier with whom she was dallying. Suspecting the liaison, the king took it from him while he slept during a hunting party and threw it in the River Clyde. On returning home the king demanded to see the ring and threatened his wife with death if she could not produce it. Languoreth asked her lover to return it, which, of course, he could not do, and in desperation she confessed all to St Mungo who,

Glasgow's original coat-of-arms.

taking compassion on her, sent one of his monks to fish in the river, instructing him to bring back the first fish he caught. When he did, St Mungo extracted the ring from the fish's mouth and sent it to the queen to restore to the king, thus saving her life.

More prosaically, the salmon may depict salmon fishing, which was Glasgow's main industry until the 18th century, and the ring may be of episcopal significance.

While the bird, the tree and the fish were legendary, the *Bell* was not. Thought to be given to Mungo by the Pope, mention of it appeared down the centuries. In 1450 Glasgow's first Lord Provost, John Stewart, left an endowment to have 'Sanct Mungowis Bell' tolled throughout the city to call the inhabitants to pray for his soul. The bell vanished during the Reformation, but a replace-

A very clever Camp coffee advertisement at the beginning of the 20th century incorporating Glasgow's coat-of-arms

ment, bought in 1641, exists in the People's Palace in Glasgow Green.

Although it was not until 1866 that Glasgow received an official coat-of-arms from the Lord Lyon, King of Arms, the common seal of the Burgh had the armorial insignia in varying designs as early as the 13th century. During their period of rule each bishop had his personal seal and the designs on the civic seal derived from those.

The Trade Mark Registration Act came into being in 1875 and a year later Glasgow City Council granted James Finlay & Co. Ltd permission to register the city's arms as a trade mark. It was a rare privilege for a commercial concern, and was allowed only because of the company's prominent position in trade. An examination of the newly-registered trade-mark revealed that the figure depicting

The Gallery of Modern Art showing the modernistic treatment of the city's coat-of-arms

St Mungo closely resembled John Muir, a partner in James Finlay. Coincidence, a touch of humour, or maybe a touch of narcissism!

Later, other companies received permission to use the coat-of-arms to promote their products, like Camp Coffee, which started life in Glasgow in 1885 and is now manufactured in Paisley. The company had a reputation for innovative advertisments and a cleverly adapted version of the coat-of-arms portraying St Mungo with a steaming cup of Camp Coffee in his hand was one of its best.

Glasgow's Chamber of Commerce, the oldest in Britain (1783) incorporates the elements of the city's coat-of-arms in its own, as does the Trades' House and Merchants' House.

Although, compared to many cities, Glasgow was late in getting its official coat-of-arms, it lost no time in displaying it around the city.

The floor of the entrance hall of the City Chambers in George Square has a magnificent mosaic example and above the Ingram Street entrance to the Trustees Savings Bank there's a particularly fine portrayal sculpted by Sir George Frampton. At midspan, facing the road, colourful representations embellish the cast-iron parapets of the Albert Bridge at the foot of Saltmarket, and at the Cathedral, graceful street lights incorporate the bird, the tree, the fish and the bell.

Appearing on the pediment of the Gallery of Modern Art in Queen Street, Glasgow's newest interpretation of its coat-of-arms is not only the most original, it's also the most controversial. All the emblems are there, but scattered on a mirrored background and more Spanish in design than Scottish. Such a modernistic treatment is totally out of place given that Glasgow's old Royal Exchange, converted from the city's oldest surviving tobacco lords' mansion, houses the Gallery.

With the restructuring of Scottish local government Glasgow received a new coat-of-arms in 1975 which differed from the old in only one major aspect — a coronet of thistles replaced the helmet on which St Mungo perched. Further restructuring brought another change in 1996 when the coronet of thistles became a castellated coronet.

Now that you have read this article about the origins of the bird, the tree, the fish and the bell, there will be nothing to puzzle over. You should have a complete understanding of the mysterious emblems surrounding St Mungo...or will you?

– 2 –
GLASGOW'S SHAMEFUL HIDDEN PAST

History books attribute Glasgow's rise in prosperity in the 18th century to its famous tobacco families — the Buchanans, the Cunninghames, the Glassfords and the Spiers, among others. However, what the books don't mention is that it was not only their dealings in tobacco and later, sugar, rum and cotton, that made them and the city prosper; it was also their involvement in the triangular slave trade between Africa, the West Indies and America.

Their ships travelled to Africa from Greenock and Port Glasgow with holds full of goods to be exchanged for hundreds of negroes — men, women and children. These slaves, who had already faced a harrowing journey from the African hinterland, were then subjected to the terrible, and often deadly, voyage across the Atlantic to the West Indies and North American ports. Those fortunate enough to survive were sold, and respectable cargoes of cotton, tobacco and sugar were bought for the voyage home.

Because of its reputation for delivering high quality slaves with a reasonable chance of surviving the rigours of the passage to America, Glasgow preferred to get its slaves from areas on Africa's Gold Coast, such as Annamabo (Guinea today). Fortunately, however, Glasgow's slavers were not always successful, as in an attempt on 7 December 1730, to carry off 140 negroes from that coast, which failed when the negroes took over the sloop, killing the mate and most of the crew.

Finding its first year's slave trading lucrative, one company, Buchanan & Simson, formed a separate slave shipping company, The Snow Pitt and Maxwell's Africa Company, named after its two ships, which could carry 500 slaves. Although the company tried to get a Glasgow master to go along to learn the ropes with the promise of his own ship if all went well, the ships, bound for Africa's Gold Coast, sailed in the hands of experienced Liverpool slaving captains. Liverpool and Bristol were the great British slaving ports, working the Annambo coast, with Glasgow placed somewhere in the midde. Frustratingly, the company's surviving

Bartering for slaves on the Guinea Coast. At one time the price of a slave averaged four yards of calico, one flint-lock musket, one 6 lb keg of coarse gunpowder, one 2-gallon keg of rum, together with a quantity of beads and brass wire.

letter-book breaks off when the ships sailed, but, as they were involved in other slaving ventures only months later, it is reasonable to assume that everything went to plan.

Most of the negroes purchased by Glasgow slavers were sold in the West Indies, only small numbers being transported to mainland America. However, at the American end slaves were often handled through trading companies — a profitable field of investment for West of Scotland merchants.

One of Glasgow's greatest merchant houses, William Cunninghame & Co., who operated trading posts for Virginia planters, prepared for its future slaving activities with superintendent James Robinson writing the following in 1767 to one of his storekeepers:

As at present you have no proper place for the reception of negroes or servants which may be sent to you for sale, you will on receipt of this get a log house built for that purpose...I leave the construction of it to you and hope you will continue it so that there will be no danger of servants or slaves making their escape out of it.

Another Glasgow tobacco giant, John Glassford & Co., operated through stores and agencies in the Carolinas under the control of Neil Jamieson based in Norfolk, Virginia. In 1764 Jamieson responded to queries from a colleague in South Carolina about the sudden and grossly inflated prices for slaves:

Negroes here have great prices all this summer, men up to £340 women up to £300, boys and girls in proportion and as there has been a law passed prohibiting importation for three years after 1 January 1765, it is thought they will sell high all next summer.

To ensure prime slaves and prime prices purchasing had to be very focused and in 1770 Jamieson's son made an agreement with various merchants, including James Buchanan and future Provost of Glasgow, Robert Donald, to purchase jointly a cargo of a hundred slaves from the West Indies, preferably between the ages of ten and forty.

Given the direct use of shipping from Greenock and Port Glasgow for the slave trade and the level of slave-trade involvement among the most powerful of Glasgow's tobacco lords, it was not surprising that slaves were brought back to the West of Scotland to serve in their masters' homes and estates. This practice was only disclosed when owners tried to recover runaways, many of whom had been treated with extreme brutality.

In May 1756, Robert Sheddon, owner of 22-year-old slave James Montgomery, placed the following advertisement in the Glasgow Courant:

Whoever takes up the said Run-away, and brings him home, or secures him, and gets Notice to his Master, shall have two Guineas Reward, besides all other Charges paid, by me.

James had been bought in Virginia about five years earlier for £56 and was to be apprenticed to a joiner in Scotland and then sold back to his Virginia master for the original price plus 1,000 lbs of tobacco. In April 1756 Montgomery was seized, bound, and

The Glassford family painted in their town home, the Shawfield Mansion.

taken to Port Glasgow to await shipment. However, on 21 April he escaped and fled to Edinburgh, only to be caught within days. At the Court of Session hearings a year later, Montgomery's lawyers argued that slavery was inconsistent with the natural rights of mankind, to which Sheddon's lawyers replied by pointing out that the British economy was quite dependent upon it, particularly so in the Caribbean. The matter was left undecided, and James died in custody in July 1757.

Bought by tobacco lord Archibald Buchanan in 1763, slave Ned Johnston was treated brutally by Buchanan's nephew. Dragged into a byre, stripped to the skin, bound with ropes and hoisted up to the joists of the house by his arms which were tied together, he was then beaten with rods till his blood ran. Fortunately, hearing Ned's cries, neighbours came to his rescue and he was set free by Glasgow magistrates.

All slave owners did not treat their slaves badly; some were quite paternalistic, albeit condescendingly, like the great tobacco lord John Glassford of Dougalston, who included a black servant in his family portrait. However, by the nineteenth century the black servant seemed to disappear from the portrait and it's hard to tell whether he was painted out or whether the frame now hides him. What is apparent is that he was deliberately hidden, much as Glasgow's involvement in the slave trade was. The portrait, painted around 1767 by Archibald McLauchlin in a room of the Shawfield Mansion, Glassford's Glasgow town house, is in the People's Palace Museum in Glasgow Green.

The American Revolution and the subsequent war with Britain disrupted the slave trade and helped to bring about the outlawing of domestic slaveholding in Scotland. In 1778 the Court of Session freed Joseph Knight saying: 'The state of slavery is not recognised by the laws of this kingdom.'

Knight was a slave brought from Africa to Jamaica and then, aged thirteen, brought to the East Coast of Scotland by his master, a partner in Webster & Wedderburn, a Jamaican trading house. Joseph and one of Wedderburn's domestic servants had a child called Annie and, when some time later Annie was packed off by the master, Joseph resolved to join her. Finding out about this, Wedderburn went to the local Justices of the Peace in November 1773 and received a favourable decision early the following year. Joseph appealed and in March 1775 the case was referred to the Court of Session. The final decision came three years later, on 15 January 1778, when Joseph was freed. Nevertheless, it was not for another sixty years that similar measures applied to overseas possessions and to the West Indian plantations at the heart of the slave system.

In the latter part of the 18th century Scots plantation holdings in the West Indies read like a who's who of the Glasgow area merchant community. The American war had turned things round. Instead of merchants treating the West Indian trade as a subsidiary to their main trade with America, the West Indies became the principal seat of their operations and a base for clandestine trade with the American mainland. Therefore, acting for Glasgow firm James Ritchie & Co. in 1780 James Anderson was trading in the West Indies with unlimited credit to purchase 'either prize tobacco, sugar, rum and even slaves if a very great bargain offered.'

Because of the increasing role of the West Indian trade following the outbreak of the American war, the West of Scotland merchant capital was increasingly drawn into the brutal core of the slave system. However, whereas in America the link was usually through shipping, the store system and advancing credit to modest slave-holding American planters in the West Indies, as well as advancing credit to planters, it was mainly through owning vast slave estates.

Although the war with France disrupted the West Indian trade, after 1793 investment in the Indies boomed. However, the exportation of the French Revolution to the Caribbean brought slave insurrection to the great plantation island of St Domingue, destroying much of the French production of sugar, tobacco, cotton and coffee, and opening the market to other suppliers. Meanwhile, the island of Grenada was showing signs of exceptional profitability and merchant capital flowed in to take advantage of the drop in French production.

Quick off the mark was the Glasgow merchant house, Alexander Houston & Co., with credit to planters rising from £184,000 in 1792 to £411,000 in 1796. However, what it had not accounted for was the speed with which insurrection in the Caribbean would spread from St Domingue to islands like Grenada and St Vincent. The 'Carib War', starting in the summer of 1795 bankrupted it, and many others, despite the government stepping in to offer £1.5 million to planters and merchants in the area. That Houston's received £240,000 signified its importance. However, apart from the economic problems arising from the company's failure, because it was so heavily involved in the slave trade, thousands of black people recently snatched from Africa were left stranded in the West Indies.

In 1806 the *Glasgow Courier*, which had hedged its bets in the 1790s, even questioning the slave-owners' account of the revolution on St Domingue, finally came out in favour of slavery, and the following year Glasgow joined the West Indian Association, an organisation formed by slave-connected cities geared towards lobbying on behalf of slavery. Despite the Glasgow Association arguing that abolition was impossible, faced with the rising tide against slavery it gradually accepted 'ultimate' emancipation at some indefinite time in the future — but not then.

Although Glasgow's Chamber of Commerce had warned the Government against being hasty in abolishing slavery in the colonies (which meant then principally in the West Indies) because of widespread pressure to act against it, the Whig Ministry disregarded the advice, passed the Emancipation Act in 1833 and paid slave owners £20 million as compensation.

To the very end emancipation remained out of the question to some pro-slavers like James MacQueen, a Grenada planter who had returned to Glasgow in 1810, and from 1821, while spearheading the local slave interest, edited the pro-slave *Glasgow Courier*. 'I do not think that any price would compensate for certain slaves if the cultivation of the estate is to be carried on', he wrote: 'There are such slaves as the boiler, the cooper, the mason and other trades on the estates that could not be replaced.'

Some planters knew when it was time to give in, like William Dobbie, the Glasgow owner of Glenhead Plantation in St Elizabeth's parish, Jamaica, who pocketed his £1,530 compensation for the emancipation of his slaves. However, a few years later he regrettably sold his plantation, as, according to him 'there was no future in it because of the extravagant demands of the negroes.'

Eventually the whole system came tumbling down, ruining many as the depreciation in the value of their estates in the Indies was so great, and thus ended Britain's involvement in the slave trade.

How other cities felt about their involvement in slaving, I don't know, but as Glasgow went to great lengths to cover up its shameful part in the evil buying and selling of human beings it seems to have been conscience-stricken. However, it could just have been that by erasing the evidence it could pretend it never happened and hypocritically, appear 'holier than thou'.

Reference material kindly supplied by Tony Milligano.

– 3 –
THE CURSE OF BOB DRAGON,
THE UGLIEST MAN IN GLASGOW

At the beginning of the 19th century Robert Dreghorn, better known as Bob Dragon, inherited the estate of Ruchill from his father, and the finest house in the city, the Dreghorn Mansion in East Clyde Street, from his uncle. His income was reckoned to be at least £8,000 a year, making him a multi-millionaire by today's standards. However, for all his wealth Robert lived in perpetual fear of poverty and refused to contribute to the poor rates until the Court of Session ruled he had to. Although blessed by wealth, in looks Robert was anything but blessed, for he was superlatively ugly. His body was tall and gaunt with an in-bent back. His head was huge and his face repulsive with an acquiline nose bent to one side of it where it lay almost flat. He was blind in one eye, squinted with the other, and had cheeks deeply pitted with pock marks. Nevertheless, for all his ugliness Bob liked to be modishly dressed, usually in a single-breasted coat reaching below his knees, powdered hair and his queue (pig-tail) ornamented with a black ribbon bow. As a finishing touch he always carried a cane when walking the streets, never hesitating to use it on urchins who got in his way. Consequently, when they saw him coming they scattered. Street urchins were not the only people to fear Bob. Glasgow mothers used him as a 'bogie man' to frighten their children into behaving. Despite being the ugliest man in town, Bob was an incorrigible lecher, his chief, if not sole amusement, being to parade the two main thoroughfares, Trongate and Argyle Street, and follow any woman who took his fancy. However, if, when pursuing one member of the fair sex another more to his liking crossed his path, he turned about face and began following the new object of his admiration.

This extraordinary feature of his character was as well known to the population of Glasgow as his ugly face and the antics of this sad man were a constant source of amusement. Although, as a rule, Bob kept at a respectable distance behind the ladies he admired, they were well aware he was following them.

Bob Dragon following some pretty girls.

Fortunately, however, they usually took it good-humouredly and treated it as a joke, often bursting into laughter, upon which Bob would give up the chase. Sometimes however, he caught up and leered at them, resulting in him being given the brush-off in no uncertain manner, including cruel taunts about his appearance. One day in 1806, aware he was nothing but a figure of fun and an object of pity, Bob decided he could take no more and committed suicide in his house.

Thereafter the Dreghorn Mansion stood empty for many a long day as it had the reputation of being a 'haunted house' where, on dark nights, Bob Dragon's ghost roamed. Eventually however, James Galloway, auditor of the Burgh Court of Glasgow, leased it, the exceptionally low rent overcoming any fears he may have had about ghosts. At first all seemed well, but soon James's daughter began to feel very scared about living in the house and pleaded with her father to leave it. For her sake he did, but very soon afterwards, in rapid succession, the whole family died — father, son and daughter. Again, the house was tenantless for many years until oil and colour merchant George Provand bought it as a home and place of business.

At that time, 1822, talk was rife about the resurrectionists (body-snatchers who violated graves and carried the bodies away for dissection) and early one Sunday morning some Saturday night revellers straggling their way home got the fright of their lives when they came across evidence of the abhorrent practice. They had taken the liberty of peeping through Mr Provand's open ground floor window and, having seen what they thought was the floor running with blood and the blackened severed heads of two children, were certain resurrectionists were in the house. What happened next proves how easy it is to incite mass hysteria.

Running to the Cross they reported their discoveries, and soon a mob was gathered outside Mr Provand's house threatening him with execution there and then for being a 'bloody old resurrectionist'. Despite the terrified old man protesting his innocence the incensed citizens smashed all his windows and began battering his door down. Alone in the house, Mr Provand tried to barricade the door, but realising it would be impossible, jumped out of a back window and made his escape up through the Stockwell. If he had not done so there is no doubt he would have been murdered on the spot as a resurrectionist, which he was believed to be. However, so hyped up was everyone that no-one thought of examining the room with the alleged bloody floor and severed heads. If they had, they would have discovered that the blood was red paint and the severed heads, two pots of black paint. What they did do was to destroy all Mr Provand's belongings by smashing, burning or throwing them in the river, except of course those items appropriated for themselves, gold, silver and copper coins, silver plate etc.

When the police were overpowered and had to run for their lives, the magistrates went for help. One ran across the bridge at Stockwell to the Cavalry Barracks at Laurieston and another to the Infantry Barracks in the Gallowgate. The infantry arrived in double quick time as did the cavalry at full gallop over the old Jamaica Bridge. The Riot Act was read, the dragoons charged with drawn

The Dreghorn Mansion in Clyde Street.

sabres, the infantry advanced with fixed bayonets and thousands of people, guilty and innocent, took to their heels and fled. Surprisingly, no-one was hurt. Next morning, Monday 18 February, the Lord Provost offered a reward of 200 guineas to anyone who would give information leading to the apprehension and conviction of the mob leaders. It didn't take long before Richard Campbell, John Macmillan, John Campbell, James Brown and John Munro were in custody. Although all were brought to trial, the case against ex-police officer Richard Campbell was more serious as, instead of aiding the police, he had incited the mob to resist them and to stone the magistrates.

All five were found guilty and sentenced to transportation beyond the seas for fourteen years. However, in addition, Richard Campbell was sentenced to be whipped through the streets of Glasgow by the hangman.

Unknown to Campbell he was to make history as the last man to be whipped through the streets of Glasgow by the last Glasgow hangman, Thomas Young, or, Tammas, as he liked to be called, whose occupation worried him so much that he rarely left his home except on business.

On 8 May Campbell was brought out of jail and lashed to a cart, which, surrounded by Dragoon Guards to keep the crowd away, proceeded to the south of the jail where Tammas laid bare

Campbell's back and with a cat o'nine tails gave him his first twenty lashes. The punishment was repeated at the foot of Stockwell Street and then at the top. Finally, the last twenty lashes, making eighty in all, were given at the crowded Glasgow Cross, the prisoner groaning and lamenting his hard fate. Harsh the punishment may have been, but it certainly showed that rioting would not be tolerated in Glasgow.

The ill-fated Dreghorn Mansion was never lived in again and eventually a warehouse took its place. As Bob Dragon was the last in the Dreghorn line, apart from putting an end to his torment, he possibly thought that by killing himself the curse attaching to the family name would fade into obscurity. That it would continue for years after his death, culminating in a riot, would never have occurred to him.

– 4 –
JOSEPH LISTER:
THE GLASGOW CONNECTION

Although out of a lifespan of 85 years, Joseph Lister spent only nine of them in Glasgow, they were the most important of his professional life as it was while employed as Professor of Surgery in the city's Royal Infirmary that he revolutionised the field of surgery by introducing antiseptics to the operating theatre.

Until Lister's day surgery had changed little since the middle ages, and although the arrival of anaesthetics in 1846 alleviated some of the horrors, it was still a terrifying ordeal for the patient. However, something else claimed more victims than the surgeon's knife — the infamous so-called 'hospital diseases', caused by germ ridden buildings and lack of hygiene. Blood poisoning, pyaemia and gangrene were the scourges of the surgical wards, and patients' chances of surviving post-operative infection were slim. Operations were restricted to limb amputation, abscess lancing and the removal of superficial cancers as even the most skilful of surgeons feared the usually fatal outcome of putrefying wounds. Venturing deeper into the body cavities was considered foolhardy, and except in cases of dire necessity it was thought wise not to tempt providence. Lister's breakthrough altered all that. Freed from the risk of infection, more ambitious surgery could be performed on parts of the body formerly beyond the scalpel's reach — the abdomen, thorax, and skull. Thus, modern surgery was born.

Shortly after qualifying in medicine in 1853 from University College in London, Quaker Lister went to Edinburgh University to spend a month of postgraduate study with the Professor of Clinical Surgery, James Syme, Europe's leading surgeon. Immediately there was a rapport between the two men leading to a lifelong friendship; and once the month was over Lister decided to remain in Edinburgh. Syme appointed him supernumerary house surgeon, a non-resident post, the duties being to assist at every operation, hand instruments, sponges etc, keep an eye on the patient, and take notes without sharing responsibility for the treatment.

Early in 1854 Lister became Syme's resident house surgeon and

Joseph Lister.

in 1855, Lecturer in Surgery at Edinburgh Royal College of Surgeons. The year 1856 was a busy one for Lister: he was appointed Assistant Surgeon in Edinburgh's Royal Infirmary and married Syme's daughter Agnes who became invaluable to him. As a doctor's daughter she knew the pitfalls of being married to one and knowing the language was able to keep his notebooks, prepare specimens and help with experiments. Also, she did not object to her home being used as a laboratory and undoubtedly without her understanding and devotion Lister would never have been able to dedicate himself so obsessively to medicine.

In 1859 Lister successfully applied for the vacant Regius Chair of Surgery at Glasgow University. However, no allocation of beds automatically went with the Chair, they had to be applied for as and when a vacancy arose in the Royal Infirmary, the city's only general hospital. Lister's first application was unsuccessful and it was more than a year before he was given charge of wards 24 and 25 in the new surgical block built in 1860, and a ward in the older part of the Infirmary.

Later, he discovered that ward 24, his ground floor male surgical ward, lay over a burial ground. Coffins, hurriedly buried, containing victims of the cholera epidemic of 1849 lay one on top of the other to within a few inches of the surface, separated from the ward by a basement area just four feet deep. Also, thousands of paupers' bodies had been piled into huge burial pits in the neighbouring old Cathedral Churchyard.

This hideous discovery only came to light when a great outbreak of deaths from 'hospital diseases' occurred in ward 23, separated from ward 24 by a passage only 12 feet wide. Mortality became so bad that the ward was temporarily closed to investigate the cause, which was believed to be a foul drain. Excavation revealed the grisly truth and the corrupting mass was treated with carbolic acid and quicklime, after which an additional layer of earth was laid on top.

Throughout his career Lister never lost his awe of, to use his own words, 'the divine mechanism of the human body'. While some doctors were devoid of compassion when treating their patients, seeing them as inanimate objects rather than as fellow human beings in need of loving care and attention, he was not one of those. He could put himself in his patient's shoes and feel their pain and understand their fear. His medical training, he believed, put him in a position to do good, and he genuinely wanted to, although sometimes the responsibility of his profession weighed so heavily on his shoulders that he was often sick with tension before serious operations.

To a man like Lister, it was difficult for him to accept that no matter how brilliant his surgery, a third of his patients would die of suppurating wounds following their operations, and, despite holding the view and teaching his students that such infection was caused by some repugnant substance in the air, he often attributed the deaths to his incompetence. Such was the ignorance of the times. However, that was about to change.

Discovering that live bacteria were the cause of disease, including putrefaction — not a chemical process — French chemist Louis Pasteur published a paper revealing that the air was laden with minute invisible microbes carried everywhere by dust. Lister didn't have much time for reading all the European scientific literature that came his way for as well as practising surgery in the Royal Infirmary he lectured in the Old College in High Street, and

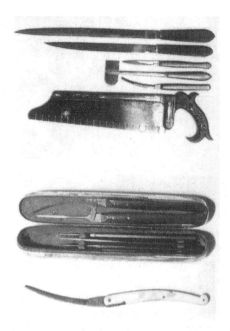

Some of Lister's surgical instruments.

it was his colleague, Dr Thomas Anderson, Professor of Chemistry, who drew his attention to Pasteur's observations.

However, Lister immediately recognised the importance of the germ theory in relation to his research into inflammation and suppuration of wounds. A lot of things began to make sense. Was it possible that during an operation the microbes in the air settled on the wound and then entered the bloodstream, poisoning the patient? But if that were so, how could it be avoided? How could the germs present in the cut or injured flesh be killed? Pasteur had destroyed them by repeated applications of heat, but obviously that was out of the question. Then he recollected reading in a newspaper that copious quantities of crude carbolic acid had purified Carlisle's evil-smelling sewers which were though to have caused the typhoid and diphtheria epidemics. Cattle grazing in fields where sewage discharged had also been sick. After the carbolic however, the smells, epidemics and cattle sickness ended.

Carbolic acid, was that the answer? Maybe if a wound was dressed with it the germs would die and the patient live? It was worth a try. Lister tested his theory in March 1865, by applying a carbolic dressing to a compound fracture (one where the bone pierces the skin leaving a wound). Unfortunately, the technique was unsuccessful. However, five months later, on 12 August 1865, he found another suitable case to experiment on. Eleven-year-old James Greenlees was admitted to the Infirmary with a compound fracture of his left shin. Lister swabbed the wound thoroughly with a piece of calico saturated in undiluted carbolic acid and then laid two layers of lint soaked in acid over the injury, overlapping it about half an inch. On top of these, to prevent the liquid evaporating, Lister placed a sheet of thin tin fixed by strips of plaster. Finally, the leg was splinted and left to heal. Six weeks later the boy walked out of the hospital, his wound and fracture healed with no sign of infection.

Lister's weekly letter to his father, written as always in Quaker form, gave chapter and verse on the case:

> There is one case which I am sure will interest thee. It is one of a compound fracture of the leg with a wound of considerable size accompanied by great bruising and great effusion of blood into the substance of the limb causing great swelling. Though hardly expecting success, I tried the application of carbolic acid to the wound to prevent decomposition of the blood and so avoid suppuration throughout the limb. Well, it is now 8 days since the accident and the patient has been going on exactly as if there were no external wound, that is as if the fracture were a simple one.

Joseph senior was very proud of his son's achievements. Not only was he head of Glasgow Royal Infirmary's Surgical Department at the age of 38. Quite an accomplishment! He had also developed a treatment with the potential to save millions of lives. Ten more cases of compound fractures were treated in Lister's wards with only two deaths, one developing gangrene when Lister was absent for several weeks and the second dying of a haemorrhage caused by a piece of bone perforating the femoral artery. Such a survival rate was unheard of, and, in 1867 the *Lancet* printed the results. Also that year Lister read a paper on 'antiseptics' to a meeting of the British Medical Association in Dublin. Its reception was mixed — scepticism, opposition, jealousy, enthusiastic support, but never indifference. Lister was constantly working on improving his treatment. The primitive dressing had defects, mainly destruction of the skin caused by the

A jar of carbolic acid the liquid used by Lister as an antiseptic in surgery which prevented putrefaction and gangrene.

undiluted acid. After much experimentation, he devised a putty made by mixing carbonate of lime with a solution of carbolic acid in boiled linseed oil, which, used as a type of poultice, did not irritate the skin or the living tissues. This new remedy completely superseded the original.

After the successful treatment of compound fractures, Lister performed more adventurous operations, one on a relative of whom he was very fond. Suffering from breast cancer, she had been refused surgery by every doctor consulted, as in 1867 surgeons still considered the risk of septic infection so great as to make such an operation futile. Although Lister had often in despair turned away other women suffering similarly, this time he felt obliged to operate, bacause if he didn't she would die. Confidence in his antiseptic treatment gave him an advantage over others, but he was so terrified of attempting an untried procedure on someone dear to him that he rehearsed it on a cadaver. His own home, not the hospital, was where he chose to operate. With great skill he removed both breast and glands. Dividing the pectoral muscles, he cleaned out the armpit as adroitly as any surgeon today. Although Lister did not succeed in preventing decomposition in the wound, the patient lived, and whereas she died three years later of a tumour of the liver, there was no recurrence of the original cancer.

The use of carbolic acid as an antiseptic in surgery was not Lister's only contribution to the world of medicine while in Glasgow. He introduced a gauze surgical dressing impregnated with boracic acid and experimented with the use of tincture of iodine to sterilise the skin. Of great importance was his discovery of an antiseptic catgut ligature which, being absorbed by the patient's tissue, did not form a source of irritation and sepsis like the silk ligature then in use. He also devised a carbolic spray designed to destroy the germs in the air before they could attack the patient, giving rise to a wry joke among his students; 'Let us spray' they would say before an operation. After a time Lister realised that the micro-organisms carried on the fingers and surgical instruments were more dangerous than those flying around in the air. He insisted on scrupulous cleanliness and frequent handwashing for all who made or dressed wounds and he was the first to devise a dressing sterilised by heat.

In 1869 Lister was chosen to fill the chair of Clinical Surgery in Edinburgh University that his father-in-law had vacated on health grounds. Despite Lister describing his nine years in Glasgow 'as the most productive and happiest of his life', he attempted to obtain another post three times. However, that could have been because under their terms of appointment all surgeons employed by Glasgow Royal Infirmary had to give up their wards and cease to hold office for at least a year after 10 years' service, then reapply — in Lister's case in 1870. Furthermore, in Glasgow, Lister's time was much occupied with routine work, starting with the early morning hospital round at 8.30. Also, as he felt his calling to be towards research his ambition being to spread out as widely as possible such discoveries as he hoped to make, the Edinburgh appointment offered an easier life, the hospital visit being at a more convenient hour, leaving more time for study. There was also the bonus of the post being permanent.

After departing for Edinburgh, Lister published a paper written while still in Glasgow, entitled 'On the Effects of the Antiseptic System of Treatment upon the Salubrity of a Surgical Hospital'. To prove the merits of his antiseptic treatment, he described, in no uncertain manner, the conditions under which he had worked in Glasgow's Royal Infirmary. He missed nothing: the cholera burial grounds beneath his wards, the filthy buildings, severe over-crowding, all were mentioned and he even went as far as stating 'my patients suffered from the evils alluded to in a way that was sickening and often heartrending, so as to make me sometimes feel it a questionable privilege to be connected with the institution.' His techniques had converted his wards from some of the most unhealthy in the kingdom into models of healthiness. For three years they had remained without the annual cleaning and upon asking the superintendent the reason for the omission, he had been told: 'As those wards had continued healthy and there was nothing dirty in their appearance, it had seemed unnecessary to disturb them.'

Naturally the Infirmary Management could not ignore such a damning attack, and they had a letter published, in the *Lancet* and the *Glasgow Herald*, categorically refuting Lister's allegations. In their opinion, which they stated was shared by those of their number belonging to the medical profession, 'the improved health and satisfactory condition of the hospital, which has been as marked in the medical as in the surgical department, is mainly attributable to the better ventilation, the improved diet and the excellent nursing, to which the Directors have given so much attention of late years.' Lister retaliated in the same journals. Very courteously and politely, he substantiated all he had published. There the matter rested, but the memory of his assault lingered long and in spite of world-wide protests, his wards in the Royal Infirmary were demolished in 1924.

When Lister went to Edinburgh it was the same old story. Not everyone agreed with his thinking, but in 1870, after he had operated to remove an abscess from her armpit, Queen Victoria gave the royal seal of approval by appointing him Surgeon-in-ordinary in Scotland: 'A most disagreeable duty most agreeably performed' she told him after her operation.

In 1877 Lister accepted an invitation to take up the Chair of Clinical Surgery specially created for him at London's King's College Hospital. Despite his international reputation, the reception accorded him was chilly, but ultimately London adopted him, as had the rest of the world.

GLASGOW CURIOSITIES

Lister became a Lord in 1897, the first doctor of medicine to be admitted into the hallowed chamber, and in 1906 he received the freedom of the cities of London and Edinburgh. Finally, on 22 January 1908, at the age of 81, he was presented with the Freedom of Glasgow, somewhat belatedly, according to many, for the city to which he had given so much was the last to acknowledge his monumental services to humanity. Sadly, ill health prevented him from attending the banquet given in his honour in the City Chambers and it was left to his closest friend Sir Hector Cameron to read to the guests a communication from him:

> I am profoundly grateful for the honour conferred upon me by the City of Glasgow. It touched a tender spot in my heart, for it carried me back to my days of youthful vigour, action and inspiring work. John Bright once defined happiness as 'congenial occupation with a constant sense of progress'. If that be true, no man was ever happier than I was living in Glasgow.

On the morning of 10 February 1912 Lister died. The world lost a remarkable man. Thanks to him surgery evolved from blood-stained frock coats and filthy surgical instruments to completely sterile operating theatres. He dispelled the myth that the 'hospital disease' haunting the operating theatres was supernatural by proving it was organic, and to his antiseptic process humanity owes an enormous debt.

EPILOGUE

When a memorial statue of Lord Lister was unveiled in Kelvingrove Park in 1924, a very moving incident occurred. After the ceremony an elderly lady stepped forward and asked permission to lay a wreath. Her name was Helen Manderson and she explained that sixty years earlier Lord Lister had operated on her wrist. She had tuberculous caries and he had devised a new operation to excise the affected bones and joints which his colleagues opposed. Fortunately, he used his own judgement and went ahead. Helen demonstrated that it had left her with a very useful hand and, although as a girl of twelve she had not understood the good that was being done, she afterwards realised the enormous debt of gratitude she owned to Lord Lister, whose skill and patience had saved her hand and possibly her life.

– 5 –
WALLACE THE FIRE DOG

Wallace the Fire Dog was a Labrador who officially became a member of the City of Glasgow Fire Brigade. His story began in 1894 when he joined the annual Lifeboat Procession as it went through Glasgow city centre. First he attached himself to a lifeboat float and then trotted alongside a horsedrawn fire appliance. Whether it was the shining brass of the engine or the two big horses, Kelvin and Clyde, that appealed to him, nobody knew, but whatever it was it made him follow the firemen back to their base at the Central Fire Station in College Street. When Wallace arrived at the Station he obviously wanted to settle in, but, recognising him, the officer-in-charge detailed one of his men to return him to his owner, a stonemason who lived with his wife and two children in South Albion Street. Wallace however, had other ideas about how his life was to be arranged. He wanted to live in the fire station and three more times ran away from home until everyone came to an arrangement that he would join the Fire Brigade on a permanent basis as its mascot. However, it was no honorary appointment. Wallace's life as a household pet was over. He was now a working dog, and one who knew exactly what kind of work he wanted to do. Immediately the alarm sounded he was out in College Street eagerly waiting for the big appliance room doors to swing open and let out the fire appliance. Wherever the firemen went, down dark alleys, along back streets or to the city centre, Wallace went with them keeping pace alongside the horses as they clattered their way, sometimes wearily, to the scene of the fire. After a while Wallace decided his rightful place was at the head of the cavalcade about thirty paces in front of the leading horses. And, if he thought that it was his yelping and barking that cleared the way along the busy streets and not the clanging of the big brass fire bell, few would have disillusioned him. In the small world of the second city of the Empire, Wallace had become a familiar and popular sight.

Old log books provide a record of some of Wallace's early fires — City Poorhouse, Gallowgate, Pawnshop, Main Street, Gorbals,

Glasgow Tramways Stables in Cambridge Street when two horses and four cows were killed, Hengler's Circus in Sauchiehall Street, a regular customer, and the waxworks in the Trongate that went up spectacularly in 1896 with six appliances attending.

On a ceremonial visit to the Glasgow Fire Brigade, an important person commissioned a pair of boots to be made to protect Wallace's front paws from wear and tear caused by the hard cobblestones of the streets. Nevertheless, sore paws or not, Wallace was out every time the alarm bell rang. He was a professional, and, ready for a quick getaway, took up his position thirty yards in front of the gaffer's bay even before the horses were limbered up.

As the city got bigger and more sophisticated the fire risks increased, with the fashionable tea rooms providing a lot of business for Wallace and his friends. Fortunately a small fire in February 1900 only slightly damaged the Charles Rennie Mackintosh décor of Kate Cranston's first tea room in Ingram Street, but in spite of the speedy arrival of Wallace and eight appliances in July 1901, her tea room at the Great Exhibition in Kelvingrove Park was gutted.

By the end of the century Wallace was so famous that a postcard with his picture and a poem headed 'A Tribute to the Dog Wallace' was published.

Firemen wha auld Wallace led,
Firemen wha's tae danger bred,
You'll be vexed when he is deid,
When yer're leader's gane.

Nicht an' day at danger's ca'
Wallace aye wa first o' a'
Tae cheer us on, through sun an' snaw,
Without a thought of fame.

For half a decade, mair or less,
He sniffed the fire afar tae guess,
Noo when he's auld in sair distress
He'll no be left alane.

We'll stick tae him until the end,
An' honour gae him like a friend,
A mair faithfu' fireman ne'er was kenned
Than Wallace.

Wallace, the famous fire dog.

There were many myths about Wallace the Fire Dog like the one about him being immune to the heat of flames. This was quite untrue; he was terrified of fire and kept well clear of it. In fact, when the firemen were going to a really large fire Wallace abandoned his place at the head of the cavalcade as soon as it got into the glow of fire. Even when it was a small fire he was up and away as soon as the first appliance began its journey back to the fire station. His role, as he saw it, was to run in front of the fire engines, not to help put out fires.

In 1900, when Wallace had been in the Fire Brigade for six years, Glasgow Corporation paid his licence as a token of his official position. In the same year the brigade moved to new headquarters in Ingram Street, described as 'the most practical, complete and useful chief central fire station to be found anywhere in the world'. A key feature was a telegraphic alarm system, specially designed by the ABC Telegraph Company of Royal Exchange Square, linking street corner fire alarms direct to the new station's watchroom. This system was a 'first', and soon towns and cities worldwide copied it.

While systems could be copied, Wallace was a 'one off'. No other city could boast of a mascot that lived for the sound of the fire alarm bell. The telephone bell and the station bells could ring as often and as loud as possible and Wallace would ignore them.

But, as soon as the alarm bell sounded he was out of the door like a flash and into the street before the firemen made a move.

Some of Wallace's admirers maintained he could tell in which district the fire had broken out by looking at the indicator flaps on the alarm board. Another theory was that he knew which route to follow because he could smell a fire miles away, a theory given some weight in the above verses written by one of Wallace's firemen friends:

> For half a decade, mair or less,
> He sniffed the fire afar tae guess...

However, the most logical explanation as to how Wallace knew which route to take to a fire is the one offered by former Chief Fire Officer William Robertson who knew more about him than anybody else. He said it was simply that the driver gave a quick signal with his whip when he was going to turn to the right or to the left and Wallace was smart enough to keep looking back as he raced along the road.

Wallace's final fire was on the night of 28 September 1902, when he led two appliances to Collins's Book Warehouse in Stirling Road. He was slow coming home and seemed particularly eager to get back to his basket in the watchroom. In the early hours of the following morning when the Trongate flap fell for a small fire at Daly's store Wallace stirred in his sleep at the sound of the alarm bell but didn't waken up. Nor did he the next morning; he had passed away in his sleep. It might be said he died with his boots on, but he didn't. He never wore those famous boots. No self-respecting dog would, especially one who had to get off to a flying start at the sound of the alarm bell. Maybe to remove the boots from the story takes away some of the romance, but it makes it more credible, and surely credibility is an important quality in such a piece of serious history as the life and adventures of Wallace the Fire Dog.

When Wallace died he was preserved and ever since has been kept on display in the main entrance to Central Headquarters, which today is at Port Dundas Road. Some say his eyes still light up when the alarm goes and it has been said the bark of a dog has been heard though no dog is there...

– 6 –
BEAU-IDÉAL OF A GLASGOW MERCHANT

Measured by any yardstick, Glasgow's Kirkman Finlay, Member of Parliament, the West of Scotland's greatest merchant and the greatest blockade runner of the Napoleonic Wars, was one of the most dynamic and impressive men of his time. Born in 1772 in a Gallowgate tenement house (then an upmarket address, but later a slum), Kirkman Finlay was the younger son of cotton merchant James Finlay. He attended the Grammar School of Glasgow where he was frequently punished, not for being a bad scholar, for he was clever, but for being 'a mischievous dog'. From school he progressed to Glasgow University. Kirkman Finlay's amazing mercantile career began when he joined his cousin Andrew Buchanan's wholesale cotton warehouse business in Stockwell Street where he learned every aspect of the cotton trade, including mechanisation, then in its infancy. As Kirkman's older brother, John, had opted for army life rather than commerce, aged 18, Kirkman joined his father at James Finlay & Co. in 1790. Sadly they didn't work together for long as his father died later that year. However, he left a thriving business for Kirkman to continue, the balance sheet showing assets of £11,784 19s 10d — not a sum to be sniffed at then.

James Finlay & Co. exported cotton goods and yarns to Europe and the introduction of new capital and partners enabled Kirkman to set up extensive trading operations at Frankfurt-on-Main and at Dusseldorf, where a branch office was opened. Business boomed and the company became the principal exporter of cotton yarn from Scotland to Germany and other parts of the Continent. As mechanisation of the cotton industry had taken over from hand spinning Kirkman bought, from his Buchanan cousins, three cotton spinning mills, which he equipped with the most modern machinery. These were Ballindalloch, Catrine and Deanston, the latter continuing under the management of the Buchanans. Being water-powered they were sited near fast flowing rivers — the Endrick, the Ayr and the Teith.

The Napoleonic Wars began in 1793 and after the battle of Trafalgar on 21 October 1805, the British Government declared the

Kirkman Finlay.

whole coast occupied by France and its allies to be in a state of
blockade. Napoleon retaliated by blockading the British Isles. All
commerce or communication was forbidden and any British goods
found in the territory of France or its allies were liable to
confiscation. This manoeuvre was intended to destroy Britain's
trade and force her to surrender. Like merchants all over Britain,
those in Glasgow were devastated. However, Napoleon's strategy
had a weakness. Europe was well behind Britain in mechanical
production and relied heavily on its exports. By implementing
Napoleon's blockade it was depriving itself of merchandise for
which there was a real demand and which could not be obtained
from elsewhere. Kirkman Finlay decided to exploit the situation.
Provided he could get the goods through the blockade he knew
there would be no disposal problem, there being any number of
disgruntled continental merchants more than willing to take the
risk. He set up depots — Heligoland in 1807 to supply the north
of Germany, and Malta in 1809 to trade with Austria and
Switzerland, via Salonica. The Baltic ports were also part of his
blockade-running network, with his Dusseldorf office its

headquarters. Upwards of 700 men were employed in Europe as agents and distributors. Often heavy losses were suffered by the seizure of ships and contraband, but there were also successes, so much so that a London warehouse was opened solely to handle the booty. By 1812 Old Boney's funds and forces were heavily committed to his Russian campaign, making it impossible to maintain the blockade. Consequently, trade between Europe and Britain gradually returned to normal.

With the war nearly over and Napoleon exiled to Elba, Kirkman visited the Continent in March/April 1814, touring extensively throughout Holland and Germany, finishing in Paris. Grim reminders of the war were everywhere. Surveying the battlefield at Hanau, 12 miles from Frankfurt, he saw where Bonaparte's tent had been pitched, the remains of dead horses, abandoned clothing and equipment and trees and houses torn to pieces by cannon shot. All evidence of the bloody battle by which the French pursued their march on Frankfurt.

By the end of the war Kirkman Finlay had not only made a fortune, he had also outmanoeuvred Napoleon's admirals — no small feat. Only a man with exceptional qualities, courage, energy, shrewd judgement and a deep knowledge of Europe could have done so. Why did he do it? Principle, profit, love of excitement, or simply to buck the system. Who knows, but being the kind of man he was, probably a mixture of all.

The year 1812 was a momentous one for Kirkman, at the peak of his popularity and power. He became Lord Provost of Glasgow, Rector of Glasgow University, President of the Glasgow Chamber of Commerce (a position he held four times) and Member of Parliament for the local burghs of Glasgow, Rutherglen, Renfrew and Dumbarton (1812-1818) — the first native Glaswegian MP for almost a hundred years. When the election result was declared on 30 October 1812, after much toasting and clinking of glasses in front of the Town Hall his jubilant supporters bundled him into his open carriage and noisily escorted it along Argyle Street to his Queen Street mansion. To mark the occasion a gold medal was struck with the inscription 'Truth, Honour, Industry and Independence'. In May 1812 Kirkman gave evidence to a Parliamentary Committee on the trading problems caused by Napoleon's blockade of British ships from European ports. Special mention was made about a fleet of six or seven hundred British-controlled merchant ships cruising in the Baltic, most of which were seized and confiscated. The value of the lost cargoes was in the region of £7–8 million. Also in 1812, wearing his Chamber of Commerce hat, Kirkman attacked the monopoly held by the East India Company, accused of greed and corruption on a grand scale for many years. A charter granted by Queen Elizabeth I decreed that all goods going to and from the East Indies had to be transported in the company's vessels, meaning that they went through the Port of London, ensuring large profits for the city. All the exotic products from the East (spices, silks, linens, indigo), reached Scotland secondhand via London or Holland.

Glasgow merchants had long since been aggrieved about the monopoly and had made repeated unsuccessful representations to Government to discontinue it. To make matters worse, countries in a state of friendship, and that included the distrusted Americans, could trade in the area. The charter was up for renewal and Kirkman and his Chamber colleagues again lobbied Government in Westminster to have it rescinded. They achieved a partial victory. An Act was passed in 1813 abolishing the East India Company's monopoly of trade with India, but not with China. That came 20 years later in 1833.

Not a man to let a little thing like a Royal Charter stand in his way, Kirkman had been sending goods illegally to the east via East India captains who had the privilege of trading privately. Nevertheless, as soon as the Act was passed, he began trading officially with India, and in 1816 the *Duke of Buckinghamshire*, a ship of 600 tons, was the first to set sail from the Clyde bound for Bombay.

To make up the shortfall caused by the lack of grain imports during the years of blockade, more and more land had been cultivated in Britain. However, when imports from Europe resumed after the war, the price of wheat fell, and, to the delight of the lower classes, bread became cheaper. But there was another side to the coin. Farmers feared ruin, upsetting the landowners, as they would be unable to collect rents, and 1815 saw new legislation through Parliament that no wheat could be imported until the price had reached 80 shillings a quarter at home. Surprisingly, Kirkman Finlay supported the Corn Laws in Parliament, the biggest mistake of his political career, for working people associated his name with dearer bread.

In 1812 ecstatic supporters had victoriously escorted him to his

Medal showing the inscription 'Truth, Honour, Industry and Independence',
struck when Kirkman Finlay became Member of Parliament for the local
burghs of Glasgow, Rutherglen, Renfrew and Dumbarton.

home. Three years later it was an infuriated mob, baying for his
blood, who gathered outside his Queen Street mansion. It took
two troops of cavalry from Hamilton and a detachment of foot
soldiers to quell the riot. To add insult to injury, to the joy and
jubilation of the jeering crowd, an effigy of him was hung on a
gibbet attached to a pillar of the Tontine at Glasgow Cross. Later
he explained his stance as based on fear that large areas of poor
land would go out of cultivation, leading to an increase in the price
of grain.

Agitation in favour of the Reform Bill was nowhere keener in
the country than in Glasgow and in October 1816, 40,000 people
demonstrated and passed a resolution to approach the Prince
Regent (later George IV) to assist in amending the Representation
and Corn Laws. So alarmed was the Government that they drafted
soldiers into the city and instructed the local MP, Kirkman Finlay,
to inform the Secretary of State on what was happening. Some
weavers took secret oaths on paper (The Treasonable Oath) to
overthrow the Government by physical force. One, Andrew
McKinlay from Calton, was arrested in February 1817 and tried for
treason in Edinburgh three months later. At the trial events took
an unexpected turn when a crown witness told the court he had
been paid to appear. The case fell apart and McKinlay was freed.

The Reform newspaper alleged McKinlay and his fellow weavers had been inveigled into putting their signatures to the paper by Alexander Richmond, a spy recruited by Kirkman Finlay, the Government being the paymaster. Very much a Tory authoritarian, Kirkman totally agreed with the Government's stance against the radicals. Nine years later Kirkman heard that the allegation was again going to rear its ugly head and with a rare lapse of judgement wrote a letter to the Glasgow press refuting past statements. In retaliation *The Reform* published a lengthy brochure leaving no-one in doubt that there was evidence to support the charges. The case was raised in the House of Lords and Earl Grey said there could no longer be dubiety — hired spies had administered the alleged treasonable oaths. It was suggested the Government wished to create political capital by making the Whiggish middle and upper classes conscious of the dangerous circumstances brewing. They thought it better the situation exploded rather than simmered. Not unexpectedly, Kirkman lost his parliamentary seat in 1818 but a year later he found another — Malmesbury in Wiltshire. However, as he did not seek re-election one term was all he served.

Because of its spectacular views over the Kyles of Bute Kirkman bought a small run-down property in Auchenwillan at Cowal in 1819. Steadily, he bought more and more of the surrounding land until he owned a large estate. He had drains installed, roads built and old farm buildings and cottages made habitable; finally Castle Toward, his new home, stood in all its turretted splendour facing Rothesay Bay amid five million trees planted on the bare slopes of Cowal.

Missing the cut-and-thrust of the political scene, Kirkman stood for Parliament in 1830 but was rebuffed in favour of Archibald Campbell of Blythswood. Undaunted, he tried again in 1831 only to be a victim of a dirty tricks campaign. His opponent, Joseph Dixon, whose wealthy father paid the bill, wined and dined influential voters and for good measure threw in a trip round Loch Lomond and Stirling lasting for days. Dixon's tactics worked. Kirkman lost the seat. In his speech on the declaration of the result Kirkman protested against the methods used to defeat him and announced his objection to the validity of the outcome on the grounds of bribery and corruption. Nevertheless, throughout the address he was calm and dignified, his tone courteous and good

Castle Toward.

humoured. Later, he presented an election petition to the House charging Dixon with 'bribery and corruption'. Unfortunately however, after long consultation, it was dismissed and Joseph Dixon retained the seat. Putting aside the disappointing end to his political career, Kirkman celebrated the withdrawal in 1833 of the East India Company's monopoly of the China Seas by despatching the *Kirkman Finlay* to Canton in 1834, the first ship to leave the Clyde for that destination. Her bell is on display in the Glasgow Chamber of Commerce.

Running such a large estate claimed more and more of Kirkman's time, and, although he was still head of the company, as he spent most of his days at Toward it seemed sensible to give up the Queen Street house and live there permanently. After several years of declining health, Kirkman Finlay died peacefully at Toward on 4 March 1842, and was buried in Glasgow Cathedral's Blackadder Aisle.

Finlay had achieved more in his lifetime than a dozen men ever dreamt of. Glasgow had bestowed upon him every honour it had. He had traded with most of the world where there was anything to buy and sell — America, Europe, Gibraltar, India and China, but never neglected his first love, the great Finlay Mills at home, which continued to trade in the face of all competition. Glasgow and the West of Scotland had lost a great man.

His obituary in the *Glasgow Herald* said he was the 'Beau-idéal of a Glasgow merchant' and made the point about the incredible growth of trade that had taken place with the Orient and how a walk to the Broomielaw would reveal ships bound for Calcutta, Bombay, Singapore, Manilla and ports all the over the East. His mercantile genius gave Glasgow an astonishing position in the Eastern and China Trade. As a final tribute to Kirkman Finlay the citizens of Glasgow raised a statue to him which today stands in the entrance to the Merchants' House. His ghost is said to haunt that establishment and has been blamed for many strange happenings. However, the consensus is that he is a friendly spirit, not a malicious one.

– 7 –
THE BALLOON MAN

Even today, when everyone is familiar with people walking on the moon and satellites circling the earth, someone making an expedition in an air balloon makes news. So, when Vincent Lunardi announced in the press in November 1785 that he intended gratifying the curiosity of the public of Glasgow by ascending in his Grand Air-balloon from a conspicuous place in the city, it's easy to imagine the excitement it caused.

Vincent Lunardi was a flamboyant young Italian who, having already made a balloon flight from Edinburgh, decided to do the same from Glasgow. Dashing, handsome Lunardi was a great hit with the ladies and skirts decorated with balloon motifs and 'Lunardi bonnets' — balloon shaped hats about 60 cms high — were fashionable accessories at the time. When Lunardi arrived in Glasgow he was very impressed with it as a letter written to his guardian in Italy shows:

> I lodged at the Tontine Hotel adjoining which is the most elegant coffee-room I have seen in Europe. The city of Glasgow is in general very neat, the streets broad, well-paved and intersecting each other at right angles. The people apply themselves with unceasing industry to commerce and manufactures which are carried to such an extent as to make Glasgow justly reckoned the richest city in Scotland. I could not help also remarking the great friendship and hospitality which subsists in this part of Caledonia...

Lunardi's 'aerial expedition' was not simply to entertain the people of Glasgow. It was to make money and he intimated in the *Glasgow Mercury* of 10 November that as soon as *two hundred pounds* had been subscribed he would fix the day of his ascension into the atmosphere. Subscribers were to receive tickets at three shillings each in proportion to the sum they subscribed. On 17 November, although the subscription money had not yet reached one hundred pounds, Lunardi named the date of his flight as Wednesday 23 November from St Andrew's Churchyard. More money was put into Lunardi's purse by exhibiting the Grand Air-balloon, 'suspended in its floating state' in the choir of the Old Cathedral for the admission charge of one shilling.

On the great day, which weatherwise was fine for the time of the year, around 100,000 people gathered to see the balloon, made of 500 yards of transparent green, pink and yellow silk, take off, among them the largest number of ladies ever seen in Glasgow, all very worried about Signor Lunardi's safety. Considering the population of Glasgow was only about 70,000 at the time, many spectators must have come from other towns. The band of the 27th Regiment entertained the crowd while Lunardi's balloon was slowly inflating and, around a quarter to two in the afternoon, when it was fully inflated into a beautiful oval shape the intrepid aeronaut appeared, dressed in a regimental uniform. To the accompaniment of the band playing a stirring march and all the church bells in the city ringing, Lunardi took his place in the car, bade farewell to his friends, and to the astonishment and admiration of the spectators 'ascended into the atmosphere with majestic grandeur'. While most people cheered and waved, some fainted, some wept and some insisted that Lunardi was in a pact with the devil and ought to be looked upon as a man reprobated by the Almighty.

The balloon rose straight up, but not with the velocity Lunardi wanted. However, after throwing out some sandbag ballast, it soared rapidly, to the admiration of everyone. A fresh gale helped it climb in a south-easterly direction and when, during this ascent, Lunardi lowered his flag a considerable distance from the balloon, the spectators were anxious, thinking the car had broken away from the balloon. In about a quarter of an hour the adventurous hero was lost in cloud, and though a glimpse or two of the balloon was seen afterwards it was impossible to view it distinctly for any length of time.

Lunardi was seen passing over Hamilton at two o'clock, so he must have been flying at the rate of 40 miles an hour. The magistrates ordered the bells to be rung and in about ten minutes he was seen passing over Lanark. During his journey a southerly current carried him along for about twelve minutes but afterwards he returned to his former course. As no news of Lunardi's landing had reached Glasgow on the Thursday, people began to fear for his safety. However, the next day they learned that he had landed in the valley of the Ale in Selkirkshire and luckily, had met a Mr and Mrs Chisholm on their way home from visiting friends. Lunardi accepted the couple's invitation to spend the night with them and left his balloon in the care of some shepherds who had watched

Vincent Lunardi's balloon.

its descent with astonishment. As Lunardi landed at five minutes to four his journey of 110 miles had taken just over two hours.

The next morning Mr Chisholm took Lunardi into Hawick where he was entertained and presented with the freedom of the burgh. From Hawick Lunardi made his way to Edinburgh but didn't stay long. He knew there was a great welcome awaiting him in Glasgow. There was, and a few weeks later he made a second ascent from St Andrew's Square which started with a near calamity. A dissenting preacher known as Lothian Tam, in his eagerness to get a close view of the flight, became tangled up in the balloon ropes and was lifted 20 feet into the air. Fortunately he was released by a jerk on the rope and fell to the ground with no serious injury. For his second trip Lunardi only reached as far as the Campsie Hills, a few miles north of Glasgow.

The first successful aerial traveller in Britain, Vincent Lunardi, died in poverty in 1806 in the Convent of Barbadina at Lisbon.

– 8 –
EXCURSION TRAIN CRASHES
AT ST ENOCH STATION

The *Daily Record* of Tuesday 28 July 1903 reported that the immunity from serious accident which had been a feature of recent Glasgow Fair Holidays was sadly marred the day before by the most appalling catastrophe in the history of the local railways. An Ardrossan train crowded with people returning to the city after the holidays crashed into the buffers at St Enoch Station killing 13 instantly and injuring 30. Later three of the injured died in hospital, bringing the death toll to 16.

The holidaymakers were returning from the Isle of Man (a favourite holiday resort of Glaswegians) and a few hours earlier had boarded the steamer *Tynwald* on the first leg of their journey home. The steamer had left Douglas just after midnight on the morning of Monday 27 July (no steamers arrived or departed from the island on a Sunday) and after a pleasant, uneventful crossing arrived at Ardrossan shortly before 7 a.m. To cope with the holiday traffic, special express trains were laid on to connect with the steamers, and as the passengers left the *Tynwald* — more than 300 of them — they piled onto the train waiting alongside the pier. At 6.58 a.m., eight minutes later than scheduled, the train departed and didn't stop until it reached Paisley, where about 200 passengers on their way to work in Glasgow got on. After leaving Eglinton Station the train crossed the Clyde viaduct and then rounded the curve leading to St Enoch Station. By this time it was just after 8.00 a.m. and the express was running 22 minutes late. Work had just been completed at St Enoch's, adding new platforms, but because of lack of space two of them, Nos. 7 and 8, were shorter than the rest by 60 to 80 yards. As the train approached the station signals showed that platform 8 was clear for it. However, instead of reducing his speed to suit the shorter platform the driver carried on as though he was heading for a longer one, with catastrophic results. The train crashed with tremendous force into the end of the platform, demolishing the wooden buffers.

Because of its weight and composition the engine was little damaged but not so the two third-class carriages immediately behind it. They received the full force of the impact. The first rebounded off the engine, its rear shooting into the air and the second, pushed by the weight of the train behind it, telescoped under the first, shattering into fragments. Cushions were torn from seats, springs were laid bare, and the walls were destroyed. All that remained was the roof which had firmly wedged itself through the first carriage. Those who witnessed the scene as the train swept into the station and crashed against the buffers at platform 8 said the sight would never be erased from their memory.

As the train approached the station most passengers were so intent on collecting their luggage from the overhead racks that they didn't notice it was travelling faster than it should have been. Nor, it appears, did those who, eager to get off it quickly to avoid the crowds, had opened carriage doors ready to jump out when the platform was reached. The impact threw those passengers standing at the open doors onto the stone platform and dashed the rest violently against the sides of their compartment. They were the lucky ones however, receiving only minor cuts and bruises. Those in the first two carriages were either killed or seriously injured. The noise of the crash echoed throughout the station and amid shrieks of terror, officials and travellers rushed to investigate. Spectators quickly gathered, all sickened by the horrific scene. Among the debris were people wedged in agonising positions and the cries and groans of the injured were heartrending.

Immediately it became apparent to rescuers that many people had died horribly, probably from 'crushing beyond the power of human endurance', as one paper put it. The *Daily Record* said: 'It would be harrowing to describe in detail the scene of blood and death which faced the rescuers, who at once set willingly to work. Mangled bodies of dead and dying, young, old, men and women, were carefully removed and laid with the tenderest solicitude on the platform.'

Messages were sent in all directions, to various police stations and to the nearest hospital, The Royal Infirmary. Responding to the call for medical help, many of the city's doctors and surgeons from the Royal hurried to the station, where they dressed wounds and set broken bones temporarily to enable the injured to withstand the journey to the hospital. The doctors were often

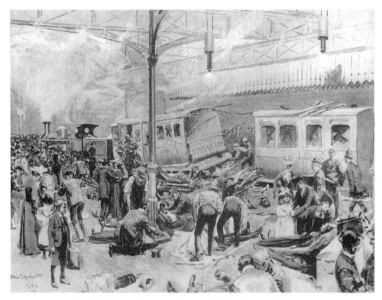

Crashed coaches on St Enoch Station's platform.

working up to their elbows in blood and it was only their experience and cool nerve that enabled them to cope with the horror. As soon as the injured passengers were extricated from the wreckage and given first aid, ambulances running a shuttle service took them to the Royal, and it says much for the efficiency of the rescue operation that by half past nine all the injured were safely in the hospital being looked after.

When the injured had been dealt with it was decided to remove the dead to a temporary mortuary, the first-class waiting room on platform 1. Unfortunately, as this was a long way from the scene of the tragedy and required a long walk through the station, every time a body was taken to it, crowds surged forward, ghoulishly trying to see the extent of the injuries. Even the ghoulish crowd however, was stunned and shocked into silence when the bodies of two children, a boy and a girl, were brought out of the wreckage together. They were Mary and Charles Wilson, although at the time their identity was unknown. What was also not known was that their parents too had been killed, their older sister Bella being the only member of the family to survive.

As news of the disaster spread through the city, hundreds of people who had received no word of relatives or friends whom they knew to have been travelling from Douglas that morning rushed to the station praying that their loved ones would be safe. Those engaged in the removal of the bodies from the wreckage to the temporary mortuary found it heartbreaking, especially when placing the little brother and sister on the floor where they lay bathed in the rays of morning light coming through the window.

Strangely, despite their horrible injuries, none of the dead was so disfigured as to be unrecognisable. Indeed, with two exceptions, their faces were not severely cut or bruised. Mutilation was not obvious, except in two men, one having had both legs severed between the knee and ankle and the other an arm and hand completely shattered and a foot terribly twisted. Soon the makeshift mortuary held 13 bodies. Never could there have been a sadder spectacle than that long row of holiday-attired dead all killed in the flush of health and well-being.

With all the bodies retrieved from the mangled train the grim task of identification began. However, with hundreds of distraught people clamouring to see if their relatives or friends were among them, the police had considerable difficulty in keeping order and eventually had to make them form orderly lines allowing only six or eight into the waiting room at a time. Many were relieved to find none of those for whom they searched among the dreadful rows of dead, but with that relief came also the realisation of the terrible sight before them and they turned away sickened and in tears. Robert James and his sister Marion were the first victims to be identified. They had been spending their holiday with Hannah Paterson who was identified later. By afternoon relatives had claimed all the bodies except one, Henrietta Anderson. All who died belonged to Glasgow except John Watson who lived in Kilsyth. The horrendous ordeal of identifying the Wilson family fell to Mr Wilson's mother who, on seeing the bodies of her son, daughter-in-law and two grandchildren, could not control her grief. She had been at home preparing for their homecoming and on hearing about the accident had rushed to the station only to find that her worst fears regarding her family were realised, with the exception of 19-year-old Bella who had escaped with a fractured leg. Tragic though all the deaths were, without a doubt the wiping out of almost a whole family was the most tragic of all, a sorrow felt by the whole city.

Later, when passengers were interviewed, the story of the tragedy unfolded. Survivor Samuel Knox told a reporter that:

> The train was a special one and was crowded. My wife and I might have gone into a compartment near the engine, but by the time I got the luggage safely in we had no time to secure a front compartment so took our seats about the middle of the train. The train had only one stop between Ardrossan and Glasgow, that being at Paisley, and it travelled at a high speed. In fact the swinging was so great that I remarked upon it to my wife. As we were entering the platform at St Enoch Station I stood up to get my luggage from the rack and just at that moment there was a violent shock. I was thrown with force against the seat, my back striking the edge of it and my wife and several other ladies fell on top of me. By the time we managed to regain our feet the train seemed to have come to a standstill. I opened the door and was preparing to alight when there was another shock and my wife and I were thrown down again.

Although injured, Mr and Mrs Knox managed to struggle onto the platform where they were confronted with an awful sight. 'One end of the second carriage was sticking right up' Mr Knox said, 'and I saw three men held fast to the seat by broken woodwork. They couldn't move and the wood had to be sawn before they could be freed.' In 1902 Mr Knox had been involved in another disaster. He had fallen from the part of the stand that collapsed at Ibrox Park and spent three months in hospital recovering. Bad luck seems to dog some people.

Among the passengers was James Brown, President of the Scottish Junior Football Association, who had a marvellous escape. He occupied a seat in the second compartment of the second carriage from the engine which was completely telescoped. 'I was dozing a good bit of the way to Glasgow', he remarked, 'and was aroused as the train entered St Enoch Station by a ratchet sort of sound. Looking around I saw everything in the compartment in indescribable confusion. Several of my fellow travellers were thrown across one another and were unconscious. For a moment I was at a loss to comprehend what had occurred, but blood trickling down the side of my face made me aware that there had been an accident. I am glad I can tell you that I escaped with my life.'

A passenger who got on the train at Paisley gave a graphic account of the scene before and after the accident. He and another workman were going to work in Glasgow and occupied a seat in the last compartment of the second carriage from the engine. He said:

> It was a smoker and contained eight men, most of whom had the appearance of having been on holiday. The train stopped at Eglinton Street where the tickets were collected and then proceeded to St Enoch. All went well and, as the train was moving along the platform many passengers lifted their luggage from the rack. Suddenly there was a tremendous crash, the door of the compartment flew open and I was thrown out onto the stone platform. On recovering I saw a terrible sight. The heads of several passengers were squeezed through the wooden panels of the carriage doors, legs protruded through the compartment floors, and hands projected through the broken windows. The cries of the injured were heartrending and the spectacle is one I will never forget. In one compartment for instance, the head of a young girl was jammed through the broken door and myself and my fellow workman tried to extricate her. However, it was too difficult a task and it was only after half of the door was torn away that the girl was freed. By that time her face was turning black and she was unconscious. In the same compartment every other occupant was dead, the passengers, men and women, lying in a heap.

Nearly all those killed instantaneously were in one or other of the compartments of the second carriage which had to be sawn through to remove the bodies. One woman who was knocked with great force against a man who had died lost her faculties temporarily and laughed hysterically as the bodies were being taken out. On telling her story a survivor, Mrs Young, mentioned seeing a lady laughing hysterically while being taken from a carriage. Michael McGheen, a passenger in the last compartment of the second carriage, believed he escaped death by being thrown through the open door onto the platform and immediately went to help, rescuing six passengers — one, a woman, dying in his arms. A man awaiting the arrival of the express said it came sweeping round the curve into the platform, travelling at a pretty fair speed. He had just been thinking that there would have to be a smart pull up for such a short platform when the engine crashed into the buffers, the first carriage rebounded and the second carriage shot under it. 'The sight was fearful' he said 'and I turned from it with a sickly feeling.'

Railway officials quickly spoke to the press about the ill-fated train consisting of 13 vehicles carrying approximately 500 passengers. They explained that the driver, 35-year-old Henry Northcott, who lived in Ardrossan, had said the brakes failed to act and he immediately reversed steam; but this failed to pull up the train in time to avert the catastrophe. They would not comment on whether he had mistaken the short platform for a longer one. Northcott, the stationmaster said, was acquainted with the platforms of St Enoch Station, having often driven between Ardrossan and the city. The police detained Northcott and stoker, Hamilton Kerr, in one of the station's offices, awaiting instructions from the Procurator-fiscal. Later, Kerr was released, but Northcott was taken into custody at the Central Police Station. Appearing in court the following morning he was remanded for 48 hours 'for enquiry as to having recklessly driven a locomotive attached to a passenger train then under his charge and caused said locomotive to come in violent contact with the buffers at the end of platform 8 whereby the first carriage was telescoped into the second, killing a number of passengers and injuring others.'

When a disaster fund was set up to help the injured and the relatives of the dead money flooded in, as the tragedy had deeply shocked the city, particularly the death of the Wilson family. Everyone's sympathy went out to Mrs Wilson for her tragic loss, and when the four coffins containing the remains of her son, daughter-in-law and two grandchildren were taken to her house at 338 Rutherglen Road, no-one who gathered to watch had a dry eye. Two days after the tragedy the family's funerals took place and after a service in Gardner Street, Partick, thousands of tearful, silent, respectful Glaswegians watched as the four coffins, conveyed in two hearses, journeyed to Lambhill Cemetery. Mother, father and children were laid in the same grave.

On 29 July the Board of Trade opened an official inquiry into the cause of the accident, headed by Lieutenant-Colonel Yorke, RE, the Chief Inspecting Officer of the Railways. Various people gave evidence, including Northcott. A station inspector said that the main rule was that a train should travel at a speed allowing the engine to be stopped by applying only the handbrake. Having witnessed the arrival of the Ardrossan train he reckoned it was travelling at 20 mph, which was excessive. During the enquiry, held in private at the head offices of the Glasgow & South Western Railway Company in St Enoch Station, Yorke visited the scene of the accident to inspect both the engine and the wrecked carriages.

A few months later Northcott was tried before Lord Kincairney at Glasgow's High Court. In his evidence he said that on entering the station he understood he had been assigned a long platform, not a short one, and by the time he realised the mistake there was nothing he could do to avert the tragedy. He explained that No. 8 was not his usual platform and, being unfamiliar with it, he didn't know it was shorter than most of the others in the station. The trial only lasted six hours. Northcott was found not guilty and set free. From the speed of the trial and the verdict, it could only be assumed that the bad management of the Glasgow & South Western Railway Company was to blame for the tragedy — an opinion strengthened when, in September of that year, investors were told that they would receive no dividend. Instead, £100,000 would be put into a contingency fund to settle any claims for compensation arising from the accident.

Before the accident, because of its excellent safety record, the Glasgow & South Western Railway was often referred to as 'The Good and Safe Wee Railway'. How tragic that because of some station renovations and lack of communication 16 people lost their lives and the railway lost its good name.

– 9 –
THE SUMMER-HOUSE ON A RAFT:
THE CLYDE FREAK SHIP LIVADIA

Although there have been many curious experimental crafts built in Clyde shipyards, the oddest of all was undoubtedly the bizarre, fantastic, turbot shaped, Russian Imperial yacht *Livadia*, built in 1880 by John Elder & Company at its Fairfield Yard. Her design was so unorthodox, her length being much less than twice her beam, and her superstructure so elaborate, that she was christened 'The Summer-House on a Raft'. The amazing freak ship was designed by Admiral Popoff, chief constructor of the Russian Navy, then 54 years of age and regarded as one of the foremost seamen and naval architects in the world. A graduate from naval school, Popoff's exceptional aptitude for strategy and naval architecture came to the forefront during the Crimean War when he taught the Russians the advantage to be got from the possession of swift steam cruisers, nine of which he built in nine months. His career went from strength to strength until he headed the Russian re-armament programme. Throughout his climb to the top Popoff was supported by a brilliant officer, Captain Goulaeff, who being well known in Britain, supervised the building of the *Livadia*.

Experimenting with round hulled ships, Popoff designed two remarkable vessels to do duty in the shallow waters of the Black Sea and the Sea of Azov, the famous 'Popoffskas'. These circular, ironclad floating gun platforms, despite poor manoeuvrability and unpleasant oscillations, had unwonted steadiness due to their exceedingly low freeboard, great breadth of beam and sloping deck immediately behind the waterline. Because of the success of the 'Popoffskas', when a new steam royal yacht was required for Czar Alexander II to replace the one lost in the Black Sea, Popoff was asked to design it along the same lines. This was mainly because, as they did not roll like conventional ships it was hoped that the Czar's wife, who was a poor sailor, would be able to cruise in the Black Sea without the discomfort and indignity of sea-sickness. That they were practically unsinkable was another important factor as it reduced the risk of nihilist activities. In fact, it was suggested that *Livadia* was being built as a sea asylum to which the Czar would resort if things got too hot for him on land, as there had been three attempts on his life. It was also believed that her steadiness would cause a revolution in passenger-ship design.

Following general enquiries John Elder's shipyard received the order, subject to a guarantee that the ship could meet the required speed of 14 knots. If it did not the Russian Government was not obliged to take her. William Pearce, Elder's chief, took the job with grave misgivings. He knew that if his company failed to build a ship capable of 14 knots, to have the contract rejected would leave the yard with an expensive, virtually unmarketable vessel on its hands. He later stated in a public lecture that many of his friends shook their heads mournfully, thinking he was a rash man, ten knots being the highest speed considered by them to be possible with such a design. However, those at Elder's were convinced that they knew what they were doing when they accepted the contract, and Pearce arranged with the open ship model basin of the Royal Netherlands Navy in Amsterdam to test the form. The report was encouraging, and further confirmation came from a tenth-full-size model tried on Loch Lomond where an average speed of over 15.75 knots was achieved. Although the *Livadia* was designed by Admiral Popoff, her lines were decided on the basis of model experiments made by Dr Bruno Joannes Tideman at Copenhagen. Dr Tideman, an engineer trained at Breda in the Netherlands and the chief constructor of the Dutch Navy, also supervised the tests at the ship tank in Amsterdam.

With a construction cost of £300,000 *Livadia* was the most expensive steam yacht ever built — and the most fantastic. Her length was 260 feet, her breadth 153 feet and although her sides rose to a height of nearly 40 feet, her draught was only 6 feet 6 inches. In profile she had a pleasant yacht-like appearance, but head on, with her very wide superstructure mounted on a hull far wider amidships, she looked almost round. She had four stumpish masts of equal length curiously situated in parallel pairs, fore and aft, with amidships between them, three huge funnels running from side to side across the ship instead of lengthwise. Enormous carrying space, the possession of a high rate of speed, and the possibility of employing her in the navigation of the shallow waters of lakes and rivers were among the unusual qualities claimed for the new imperial yacht.

A few days before *Livadia's* launch Captain Goulaeff made her the subject of a lecture in the Fine Art Institute in Sauchiehall Street. He described her as a 'palace' built on an enormous steel turbot, or raft, and, being so novel in every aspect, her construction showed a wonderful combination of ideas and foresight, proving the extraordinary amount of inventive genius in the mind of her designer. 'Although she might have been a bit narrower to suit the taste of most people' he said, 'the breadth of 153 feet cannot be regarded as being too great if we bear in mind the main object of her design, namely, the desire to secure the greatest steadiness.'

The turbot, or understructure, of the vessel was in fact the ship proper into which were fitted the engines, boilers, pumping arrangements, coal bunkers, stores — in short, everything required for propulsion and safety. This part of the ship, Goulaeff explained, was 'the most important and revolutionary feature of her design. It will act as a breakwater to the hull proper, maintain the absolute stability of the vessel in any weather, and make "mal-de-mer" unknown.' The strength of the steel superstructure rising over the turbot part of the vessel was designed to form a support for the palace and deck-houses, to raise them so much above the level of the sea as to prevent anything but spray reaching the parts intended for the use of the imperial party. Deck houses almost covered the main deck, which had another above it equally spacious and almost as fully covered by saloons. The main deck had accommodation for the crew forward, the officers aft, and, away from the heat and smell of the engines and galleys, apartments for the emperor and cabins for his entourage. In the upper deck, in front of the funnels was the bridge, and behind them, rooms for the Grand Duke Constantine and the ship's captain.

Corridors in the imperial part of the ship were luxurious and spacious, with electric lighting and marble flooring, very much like palaces on land. A reception saloon, with headroom of 12 feet, greater than in any other ship, had Louis XVI décor and an illuminated fountain surrounded by a bed of flowers. The drawing room was furnished in Russian style, the other rooms in modern English. Glasgow-born architect, William Leiper, was responsible for all the interior decoration, which accounted for a good part of the vessel's cost. In those days European royalty met frequently, using their beautiful, extravagant and large sea-going craft as

The Livadia *and Admiral Popoff.*

mobile homes which is why *Livadia* was designed as a water palace. The electric lighting on the yacht was designed and supervised by Lieutenant Rimsky-Korsakoff — said to be the first to introduce electric lighting into British shipyards so that the men could work at night.

Although very much a 'mystery ship' to the public, the *Livadia* excited curiosity far beyond the Clyde, with nearly all the world's leading naval designers visiting Elders to see such a bizarre ship being built. She was to be launched at Fairfield on Wednesday 7 July and never was there more demand for tickets to view a launching ceremony. There were privileged guests and newspaper correspondents from every maritime part of the country, even from the Continent and America. William Pearse had astute ideas for publicity and his friend Frederick Wicks, editor of the *Glasgow News*, had been useful in broadcasting to the world the revolutionary design of the new wonder yacht which was to abolish sea-sickness and make the playing of billiards possible on the stormiest seas. Such was 'Livadia fever' in the city leading up to the launch, that small boys had the name 'Livadia' in gold on the ribbons of their navy caps, completely usurping the legends 'HMS Devastation' and 'HMS Temeraire' fashionable the year before.

On the great day enormous crowds gathered along the south bank of the Clyde at Govan to witness the historic occasion. The Grand Duke Alexis of Russia represented the Czar, and Admiral Popoff was there with the Duchess of Hamilton, wife of Scotland's premier peer and hostess to the Russian visitors. There was no hitch in the launching of the *Livadia*, named after a town near Yalta on the south Crimean Coast famous for its Russian Imperial Palace, a favourite resort of Czar Alexander. After the launch, a four-hour civic banquet was held when the Grand Duke praised Glasgow as 'the centre of the intelligence of England'.

The *Livadia* was ready for trials in the Firth of Clyde in October and under pressure averaged 15.725 knots. At full speed nearly 200 tons of coal per day were burned. As she had met all requirements Captain Goulaeff accepted her on behalf of the Russian Imperial Navy. When she sailed for the Black Sea in November, the Clyde was more concerned about her fate than that of almost any other ship that had left its yards since the days of the *Comet*. Weeks passed with no news, until it was known that, after a stormy passage, putting the severest test on her claims to exceptional stability, the *Livadia* had put into El Ferrol in Spain for minor hull repairs.

She had met a gale in the Bay of Biscay and, whilst rock steady as far as rolling or pitching was concerned, her flat bottom and extraordinary beam had terrific strains put on them which would have broken the back of any such vessel with less superb workmanship on it than the Clyde could guarantee. She sank by the head when butting into heavy seas and waves washed over her fore and aft, in no way repelled by her 'turbot' breakwater. It was plain that if the Czar had a passion for billiards and his wife wanted to avoid being seasick, their new yacht was not going to be very helpful. On leaving El Ferrol the *Livadia* went round to the Mediterranean, was next heard of in the Black Sea, eventually reaching her destination, Sevastopol.

Czar Alexander II never set foot in his new yacht, the Nihilists finally got him and he was assassinated by a bomb in March 1881. His wife, after one experience of sailing in *Livadia* said she would never go to sea in her again, as she believed that the 'summer-house' part would come adrift from the 'turbot'. The *Livadia* was condemned as a failure and handed over to the Navy, who renamed her *Opit* ('Experiment'). However, as she was useless as a sea-going ship, the magnificent furniture and fittings were removed to the Naval Club at Sevastopol, the engines put into three new gunboats and the ship herself used as a store ship, a hulk for the crews of ships in dry dock. She was also used as an engineering and submarine mining school. Eventually her hulk was left to rot on Sevastopol beach until 1926 when she was sold to shipbreakers.

What an ignominious end for the *Livadia*, 'The Summer-house on a Raft', the ship that was meant to revolutionise shipbuilding, but ended up a joke. There are two good models of *Livadia*, one in Glasgow's Transport Museum, the other in the Naval Museum in St Petersburg. The plans, all in remarkable and immaculate condition, are in the Ships Plans and Technical Records Section of the National Maritime Museum, Greenwich, held at the Plans Stores at the Royal Brass Foundry at Woolwich.

– 10 –
THIRTEEN DEAD IN GLASGOW FIRE

Twelve girls died when trapped in a fire at Grafton's fashion store in the centre of Argyle Street on Wednesday 4 May 1949. One who jumped from the burning building was killed and 19 were rescued and taken to hospital. It was Glasgow's worst outbreak since 1905, when 20 people lost their lives in a fire in a model lodging house in Watson Street, near Glasgow Cross.

Thousands of passers-by watched as customers rushed from the store and employees made their escape from the building. So dense were the crowds that mounted and military police had to control them, as they were stopping the fire appliances and ambulances getting through. Traffic congestion spread to the neighbouring streets with long lines of tramcars and motor traffic held up, and for a period practically the whole of the city's through-traffic was affected by diversions.

When Section Officer Jackson answered the fire alarm call to the corner of Argyle Street and Miller Street he found it hard to tell where the fire was, as everything was blacked out from Stockwell Street. 'I was directed to the Argyle Cinema by some civilians' he said, 'and immediately told the manager to get everyone out. There was a good number inside. I was surprised, but they came out very quickly, some demanding their money back.' On realising that the fire was actually next door at Graftons, Jackson rushed to the front door but was driven back by the terrific heat. When Firemaster Chadwick arrived at the fire some of his men were using a 60-foot turntable ladder to bring people down from the roof of the cinema. However, realising that hoses were making no headway in controlling the fire, he ordered the ladder to be brought back into the street so that he could get some jets on to the top of the blazing building. Despite the turntable ladder being used as a water tower and hoses playing on the front and rear of the building, because of the intense heat and suffocating black smoke, it took fireman 40 minutes to fight their way into the ground floor. Ninety minutes after the start of the fire, the first victims were found and over an hour later firemen reached the rest. They all appeared to have died of asphyxiation. Most of the bodies were found together on one floor as, with all escape ways being screened by flames, the terrified girls had raced to the upper floors to make a desperate bid for safety.

Before firemen reached the blazing four-storey building, men and women workers were risking their lives rescuing colleagues and customers. There were about 80 girls, mostly administrative staff, in the building when the fire was discovered by window-dresser, Olga Tempini. 'I opened the door of the small room beside the lift shaft which we window-dressers called the "cubbyhole" and smoke poured out', said Miss Tempini. 'I shouted "Fire" and that raised the alarm. In a minute everything seemed to be ablaze, but, with some of the others, I had time to go up and down once in the elevator warning members of the staff.'

Grafton's managing director, who was in his office on the third floor, said that when he ran downstairs the flames seemed to blow up suddenly. He ordered everybody out, and while customers and some staff rushed to safety in Argyle Street, others, cut off from the main entrance, escaped at the back. An employee who was on the bottom floor when the fire broke out immediately made his way to the upper floors and was able to help several people escape. By then, although the building was an inferno and his hands were badly burned from his rescue work, he managed to escape and was taken to the Royal Infirmary. After being treated he returned to the shop to help further.

The scene, as men and women appeared through flames and smoke at the upper-floor windows was described to a reporter by an employee of the Cable Shoe shop directly opposite Graftons:

> Rushing into Argyle Street, I was horrified to see a girl drop from the second floor of Grafton's to the pavement below. I ran over to see if I could help her but ambulance men quickly dealt with her and took her to hospital. Looking up at the building I then saw two men and five girls coming out of a top floor window. They perched on a narrow ledge running along the face of the building and, clutching a higher ridge with their hands, moved inch by inch towards the Argyle Cinema roof next door. Crossing the roof, they got down to the slates of a lower building adjoining. There the girls, helped by their two men colleagues and firemen, were roped and lowered down a fire escape.

The two men who led the girls to safety to the detriment of their own lives were ex-paratrooper, Solomon Winetrobe, manager of Grafton's stock and invoice department, and his assistant Mr Platt. They had climbed through a window on to a sloping ledge, and while Winetrobe had stayed where he was Platt edged his way on to the roof of the Argyle Cinema. There was some hesitancy about the girls coming through the window, but Winetrobe was able to reach it with his left hand and with his right hand he grasped a vertical rone pipe. He passed the girls below his body along to Platt, and although smoke was coming out of the window he succeeded in getting five girls out. The last to leave was a greatly distressed Mrs Sloan. At the enquiry Winetrobe was asked if Mrs Sloan had practically fallen between his legs. 'Yes, but I managed to grip her between my knees and pull her up again', he answered. At the finish of Winetrobe's evidence the Sheriff asked him: 'When you were getting the girls were you dependent on the rone pipe?' 'Yes', Winetrobe replied. Sheriff: 'If that had gone, that would have been you?' 'Yes', Winetrobe answered.

Nancy Charnley of Coatbridge, aged 16, the girl who jumped from the building, died on the way to hospital. Policeman Ernest Sinclair rescued five girls from the fire. Jumping from a tramcar he ran into the shop, got through the flames and smoke to where girls were cornered, and one at a time carried them out of the building. 'I shall never forget the scene in that shop' he told a reporter.

With handkerchiefs tied over their mouths to protect them from the choking smoke, employees of neighbouring clothing stores worked feverishly to remove stocks and shoppers in nearby premises, locked away from entrances fronting Argyle Street, had to leave from side exits. As firemen in oxygen masks were battling to reach the trapped assistants, a staff supervisor was trying to take a roll-call of girls mustered in the street to see exactly how many were missing. However, as the lunch-hour was just ending when the fire broke out, it was not known how many employees were in the store and the roll-call was considered incomplete. Sixteen-year-old Jessie McKenzie and her sister Jemima, aged 18, from Cumbernauld both worked in the shop. Jessie, injured while escaping from the fire, went home after being treated at the infirmary, still anxious about her sister whom she had not seen after the fire started. Jemima had not returned home and later her brother identified her as a victim.

Girls being rescued from the fire.

Victim Wilhelmina Clemenson, aged 21, had called on her sister, Mrs Hay, at one'o'clock on the day of the fire to tell her that their father was in hospital. Shortly afterwards, Mrs Hay saw the fire and made enquiries about her sister. At the time she could not get information, but later she learned that her sister had died.

Thousands of people, led by Lord Provost Warren, mourned at Glasgow Cathedral on Sunday 9 May for the 13 girls who died in the fire. Nearly 2,000 crowded into the Cathedral, 5,000 more stood outside and hundreds walked across to the Barony Church where the Revd Roy Sanderson gave an impromptu memorial sermon. The first of the thousands of mourners streamed into Cathedral Square an hour and a half before the memorial service began. Finally a half-mile queue five-deep stretched from the gates down John Knox Street into Wishart Street and when the Cathedral doors opened police had to control the crowd. Relatives and workmates of the dead girls sat in reserved seats in the nave. The Lord Provost and the city magistrates sat in front of 30 uniformed firemen, some of whom had fought the fire. During the service three women, sobbing bitterly, rose and stumbled out of a side exit. Later the entire congregation stood with bowed heads for two minutes and outside the crowds waited in the chill dusk until the service ended.

At the end of the three-day fatal accident enquiry the verdict of the jury, announced to a hushed, crowded courtroom, was that the girls who perished inside the building died of carbon monoxide poisoning, burning and asphyxia. It was also recorded that the fire originated from an 'undiscovered cause' in a small compartment underneath the staircase next to the lift shaft, and that within a few minutes it had swept through the building.

Although at the enquiry the Fire Brigade was praised for its efficiency, in his address to the jury Grafton's lawyer, John Cameron KC, accused it of having 'some lack of that dash and undaunted devotion to duty known in the past and had the same determination, courage and skill been displayed by it as was displayed by Winetrobe and Platt, you and I would not have been brought face to face today.' Cameron asked Section Officer Jackson, whose detachment was the first to arrive at Graftons, why the turntable ladder had been used as a water tower instead of running it up to the windows of the top storey of the building in an attempt to save human lives instead of property. 'Is it not your first duty as a fireman to rescue people trapped in blazing buildings before you actually attempt to put out the fire?'. Jackson admitted that it was, but 'in this case I had no idea there were still people in the building. In any case, owing to the presence of overhead live wires, it was impossible to pitch the ladder against the wall of Grafton's.'

Fireman William Baillie explained the difficulties his detachment had had with the turntable ladder and the overhead wires. 'Looking up from the street through the intense smoke, I saw a woman hanging on to a ledge. There was a man holding her by the arm. We swung our ladder into position and I managed to help the woman on to the roof of the Argyle picture house. I stepped on to the roof too but it was impossible to keep the ladder in that position and it was withdrawn.' On being asked by Assistant Procurator-fiscal Robert Macdonald if he could have got into Grafton's premises when he went up on the turntable ladder he said it was impossible because of the terrific heat and the awkward position. 'I had to creep between live wires to reach the ledge where the woman was hanging' he explained.

Baillie was then questioned by Cameron who, showing him a photograph taken while the fire was in progress with the turntable ladder close to Grafton's shop, asked if a sign of terrific heat is the breaking of glass? Baillie: 'Yes'. Cameron: 'You see, in this picture the windows are not broken. It does not suggest great heat, does it?' Baillie, 'I was up there. I should know.'

Firemaster Chadwick told the court of the great danger to his firemen if their ladders met the street's 600-volt overhead wires and said he asked a police officer to get the current switched off. He also said that dense smoke and fumes made an entrance into the building impossible, even with the use of breathing apparatus, and on being asked by Cameron if it had been possible to put a turntable ladder against a ridge could he have gained access and get people out he replied: 'It would have been impossible at the time I arrived. I think every attempt was made to get into the building.' After the fire was under control Chadwick said he had inspected the fire escape doors and found those on the second and ground floors padlocked.

In his address to the jury, Assistant Procurator-fiscal Macdonald said:

> It may occur to you that the absence of an adequate warning system in these premises contributed in no small degree to the unfortunate sequel. There were escape doors leading from each floor. You will require to consider what was the purpose of locking these doors. These locks and padlocks completely negatived the safety doors and turned them into something resembling a trap.

On giving its verdict the jury criticised the owners of Graftons by stating: 'Owing to the inflammable state of the stock and to the extreme youth of many employees, specific precautions should have been taken against an outbreak of fire, e.g. fire extinguishers and an adequate warning system.' It expressed sympathy to the dead girls' relatives, most of whom, in heavy mourning, were in court, and singled out for commendation Mr Solomon Winetrobe and Mr Platt for their heroic rescue operations. Mr Winetrobe later received the George Medal for his bravery.

– 11 –
THE ONLY MAN IN GLASGOW WHO COULD PROVE HE WAS SANE

The Clincher, alias Alexander Wyllie Petrie, was one of a long line of Glasgow characters who many considered to be a halfpenny short of a shilling. A complete individualist, he was unable to conform to convention, believing he had the right to say openly what other people thought privately, which he did from street corners and in his broadsheet *The Glasgow Clincher*. He saw himself as a brilliant, original thinker and a leader of men whose destiny was denied him by lesser beings in positions of power. His nickname came from his declaration that by virtue of a silver cell in his brain he could clinch any argument. Despite the impression he gave, Petrie was actually sharp-witted, extremely egotistical, and even had a certificate proving that he was the sanest man in Glasgow. He was also a handsome man and dressed impeccably, if somewhat flamboyantly. In later years he boasted a white beard, top hat, lilac waistcoat and a frocked coat with a flower in its lapel.

The Clincher, born in 1853, was a barber to trade and first attracted public attention when he had a barber's shop in George Street opposite the City Chambers. It was common for him to leave a customer half-shaved while he ran out of the shop to follow a procession or a fire engine. Eventually he lost his shop licence because of his bizarre behaviour and complaints from adjacent shopkeepers who said he was ruining their businesses. Another reason for the loss of his licence could have been that a prominent bailie bought some of his patent hair restorer — Petrie's Golden Petals — and finding it did not cure his baldness, went back to complain. To mollify him Petrie offered him a free shave. Halfway through it however, the demon barber asked the bailie: 'How would you like to have your throat cut?'. The half-shaven bailie bolted!

Being shopless gave the Clincher plenty of time to spare, and in 1896 he started treating the crowds in Exchange Square to tongue-lashings against the establishment, mainly directed at his constant enemies, the police, and particularly Glasgow Corporation. However, yet again, because he was interfering with their trade, nearby shopkeepers objected and complained to the police. He then decided to write, print and publish a broadsheet dedicated to righting all that he considered wrong, and the first issue of *The Glasgow Clincher*, which claimed to clinch any argument, hit the streets in July 1897, price 1d. In his first leader as editor he said, 'I shall apologise but once for all'. He had a high opinion of his skills. 'Since the battle of Bannockburn they have been wanting a real newspaper editor in this country. They have got one now, and he is the Clincher that clincheth.'

The Clincher distributed his paper himself, and quickly found readers eager for its witty, often scurrilous content, especially when it was aimed at the integrity of the city fathers. That he also gave his enemies a vocal lambasting when selling it added to its attraction. Petrie's paper unmercifully criticised everyone in authority, and his arch enemy in the press became the editor of the *Evening News* when that gentleman ridiculed the Clincher for offering himself as prospective Parliamentary Candidate for Kilmarnock and District, promising voters that they would be electing a future Foreign Secretary.

In the streets Petrie was a great attraction. People thronged to hear his latest broadside against officialdom and when the city's most successful businessmen formed the exclusive Forty Club, the Clincher's comment was, 'An aptly chosen name indeed. All they need is Ali Baba.'

As the laws of slander meant nothing to the Clincher it was said that many a man paid far more than 1d for a copy of the paper on the understanding that he would not be pilloried in it, thereby leaving his reputation intact — a statement I find hard to believe, as Petrie didn't care what anyone thought about him and certainly didn't care what he said about anyone else. No-one was sacrosanct. In one issue of his paper he wondered where a certain magistrate spent some weekends, and added that no doubt his wife must wonder too, informing the lady that her husband was as false as his teeth. Commenting on a newspaper advertisement for sweaters inserted by a well-known clothing manufacturer, he advised his readers that the only sweaters were the exploited work force. Another time in his role as a defender of public morality he called a noted Glasgow clergyman 'a religious randy'.

Alexander Wylie Petrie, the 'Clincher'.

Although the public loved The Clincher's exposés, obviously those at the receiving end didn't, and as no-one knew who would be next, obviously something had to be done about him. Inevitably the police became involved and he found himself appearing in court usually charged with obstruction of the public highway. However, to a man like the Clincher the court proceedings, with fines of up to 40 shillings, only added fuel to his fire, and his accusations became more scurrilous than ever. His vendetta with the police assumed the proportions of guerilla warfare, for he was convinced that they were in league with the Corporation who was ordering them to harass him at every opportunity. Once he was taken into custody by a PC Milligan and charged with using obscene language. Everything seemed straightforward for the police until the trial when the Clincher triumphantly produced three witnesses who refuted the constable's testimony. The charge was found not proven!

A few days later Milligan arrested Petrie again, this time for disorderly conduct. However, when the case came to court and Milligan took the stand, Petrie objected loudly to a well-known perjurer taking the oath and accused the police of kicking the only truthful witness — a boy who helped sell his paper in the street. He was fined 40 shillings and cautioned for the next six months.

His next visit to court was when Bailie Hunter fined him and told him in no uncertain manner to reform, which of course went in one ear and out the other. In the next issue of his paper Petrie protested against the 'obvious injustice inflicted on a decent upright citizen' adding, about Bailie Hunter, 'I will say nothing about him meanwhile if he learns to go home to his wife at a reasonable time of night, because decent men's daughters do not wish to be annoyed by lascivious men while I get nothing but abuse from the lowest hounds in Scotland.' Some idea of saying nothing!

Petrie continued tormenting the city officials and representatives until at last enough was enough, and on 25 September 1897 he was arrested and, after an examination by Police Doctor John Lothian, committed to Woodilee Lunatic Asylum. The statements of two doctors who examined him on admission were at variance. One said: 'This is a first attack and is of uncertain duration…he is dangerous to others'. The Clincher was never violent. The other was fairer: 'He says the people who put him here want to get rid of his paper which is too candid for them. He says the object of the Clincher is to get rid of the Whisky Magistracy of Glasgow.' A story circulated that while Petrie was in the hospital he was found staring at a clock and on being questioned he asked the doctor, 'Is that clock right?'. The doctor took out his pocket watch, examined it officiously and answered 'Perfectly'. 'Well, what's it doing in here?' said Petrie.

Petrie's incarceration provoked a storm, with letters pouring into the papers demanding the immediate release of as sane a man who ever suffered the tyranny of the Glasgow police system stating, 'It is a glaring injustice to a courteous, harmless barber and if a man is to be incarcerated for eccentricity then half the population of the city should be there with him.' Grateful though he was for the public's support, Petrie had no intention of staying locked up and he found two independent doctors to certify him sane, obtaining a certificate as proof. When he was released, the November issue of his paper appeared with a copy of the certificate on which he based his claim to be the only Scotsman to be certified sane.

THIS IS A CLINCHER

THE EDITOR IS CERTIFIED TO BE OF PERFECTLY SOUND MIND

121 Douglas Street,
Blythswood Square,
Glasgow
Glasgow 5th November, 1897

I hereby certify, on soul and conscience, that I have this day professionally examined Alexander Wyllie Petrie, residing at 3 Randolph Terrace, Mount Florida, and that I am of the opinion that he is of perfectly sound mind.

[Signed] D. Campbell Black, M.D. F.R.S. Ed. etc.
Emeritus Professor of Physiology,
Anderson's College School.

Sales of Petrie's paper went up, and to the delight of the people of Glasgow he lost no time in flaunting himself and his certificate in front of the City Chambers. His certificate was also put to good use at public meetings. He would tell the audience that he had been in a mental institution; and then, brandishing it, he would say he was the only sane man in Scotland. 'I have a certificate to prove it' he would say, and then, pointing to his audience, ask: 'Have you?'.

The Clincher got great mileage out of his stay at Woodilee, and if he wasn't talking about it he was writing about it. One announcement in *The Glasgow Clincher* said, 'Alexander Wyllie Petrie, barber, vocalist, instrumentalist, Scottish carpet weaver, ladies hairdresser, dramatist and literature editor — for this I am declared insane.' Regular features and columns included 'Woodilee Wanderings' and 'Out on Bail', and the Clincher called upon a weird variety of correspondents to continue his fight against the establishment, especially the police:

Our Shellfish correspondent says, 'The only difference between a camel and a policeman is that a camel can work nine days without drinking, and a policeman can work nine days without working.

With remarks like, 'Why should the public want to spend money visiting Bostock's famous Zoo and Circus when they have a bigger zoo and definitely a better circus in the City Chambers?', it was obvious Petrie would be in bother again with the police, and eventually his protests to magistrates during various court attendances led to warnings that he would be fined for contempt of court, if they didn't stop. On one occasion when he was arrested, finding himself face-to-face with Dr John Lothian, who had committed him to Woodilee, he immediately said to him, 'You made a fool of yourself once before — are you going to do it again?'.

In the March 1901 issue of his paper Petrie printed a letter he had addressed to His Majesty King Edward VII, appealing against his police court convictions and listing a catalogue of injustices against himself committed by the Corporation, the police and the businessmen of the city. He also demanded that his barber shop be given back to him. The April issue carried a further letter to the King with a reprimand for not replying to the first and saying that his mother, Queen Victoria, was foolish in conferring a knighthood on Thomas Lipton, the industrial pirate. Petrie's disrespect for the famous was renowned. Lipton was 'a pork ham slasher'; Sir William Bilsland was a 'successful scone grocer' and Harry Lauder was dismissed as a 'comic singer with a crooked brain to match his crooked stick'.

Petrie applied for the post of Chief Constable of Glasgow in 1902, printing his application in his paper in full:

> I shall concentrate my mind not on the manufacturing of crime, but endeavour to the best of my ability to suppress crime so that the police economy of Glasgow shall in future be a terror to evildoers from the Lord Provost down to the most humble Corporation official. I shall not persecute or oppress decent people as has been done in the past, neither shall I insist in putting a philosopher in jails and lunatic asylums to please the scientific pickpockets of the city. Yes, as Chief Constable I shall praise those who do well. I shall take no tips or perquisites of money, jewellery, clothes, boots, bread, beef and beer. No. £1,000 a year will keep me and mine comfortably, and not only so I will be able to help those who are in need through no fault of their own. Trusting you have the wisdom of the wise to outvote the folly of the fool so I shall be declared your elected one. I enclose testimonials from my wife and the medical faculty.

He never got the job.

Although it's hard to believe, throughout all his turmoils Petrie managed to support a wife and family. I shudder to think what his wife thought about his goings-on, but with a man like Petrie, I don't suppose he took a blind bit of notice of anything she may

T H E
✠ G L A S G O W ✠
CLINCHER.

The masthead for Petrie's broadsheet, The Glasgow Clincher.

have said. He would have done exactly what he wanted to do. At one time his sayings were on every tongue, and the following little story shows how highly rated the Clincher was in Glasgow. At the beginning of the century, when Samuel Chisholm was Lord Provost of Glasgow, during a lesson on general knowledge a school teacher told his class that Prime Minister Mr Campbell-Bannerman was the first citizen of the United Kingdom and then asked, 'Can anyone tell me who is the first citizen of Glasgow?' A bright boy immediately put up his hand, 'Please sir', he said, 'The Clincher!' So much for Samuel Chisholm!

Throughout the Boer War Petrie constantly harangued the War Office about its bungling attempt to conduct a military campaign, saying he could do better with a battalion of the Boys' Brigade. He also said that the only general of any worth was General Booth of the Salvation Army. When it came to the next war Britain was involved in (the First World War) Petrie for once was not at odds with the powers that be; he actually held meetings advocating enlistment in the forces. Despite his altercations with members of the cloth, Petrie was a devout Christian. That, however, did not stop him enjoying scandalising passing ministers by shouting, 'Sensation in heaven, the Lord's not arrived yet.' Occasionally he redeemed himself for his outbursts by stating, 'The Proverbs of the Bible will do more good for generations to come than The Boys' Brigade rifle.'

Alexander Wyllie Petrie died in the Victoria Infirmary on 21 May 1937. At his funeral a newspaper report said that only a few stragglers walked behind his daughters. When the coffin had been lowered into its grave, one daughter recited the 23rd Psalm and then thanked the strangers for paying tribute to her father's memory.

This quiet ending was not what Petrie had envisaged. His paper in February 1899 had predicted something rather different. 'They were tolling the bell the other day', he wrote, 'and a gentleman seriously enquired: "Is the Clincher really dead?". 'No', the man replied, 'the Clincher will never die, but when he passes away the raw grain whisky syndicates bailies will ring their old metal bells all over Glasgow.'

For a good while before his death the Clincher seemed to vanish from public life. His obituary in the *Glasgow Herald* said that this was because of ill health, and added, 'When he emerged he was an old man with a long, grey beard...tall and carrying himself erect despite his four-score and more years...He did not harangue the passers-by as of yore, but he was ever ready to engage in chaff.'

So ended the Clincher, one of Glasgow's most colourful characters — a self-opinionated extrovert some thought eccentric, some thought insane. Well, eccentric or insane he may have been, but he was also courageous, if foolhardy. In spite of all the trouble he gave himself and all the enemies he made, he never compromised. If he thought he was right, which of course he always did, he fought to the bitter end. He felt his role in life was to speak out against hypocrisy and civic and business wrongdoing as a kind of self-appointed ombudsman, which he certainly did.

– 12 –
THERE IS NO TEA LIKE CRANSTON'S

That Glasgow was the birthplace of the tea room, there is no
dubiety. There is some, nevertheless, about who pioneered it,
the honour invariably going to the much-written-about Kate
Cranston whose fame came not so much from the excellence of
her tea rooms, but from their distinctive décor and furniture
designed by Charles Rennie Mackintosh. However, it shouldn't. It
was her brother Stuart who came up with the concept. Kate just
followed in his footsteps, albeit so successfully that she eclipsed
him.

Stuart Cranston was born in 1848 into a family of hoteliers, his
father George being the proprietor of several hotels in Glasgow's
George Square. His entry into the tea trade came about through
the influence and advice of a regular guest at his father's hotels,
Arthur Dakin of Richard Twining & Co., London, who persuaded
him to accept a lowly position as invoice clerk with Wright, Napier
& Co., wholesale tea traders. In winter, when flakes of snow
whirled about the warehouse dispatch desk where Stuart sat trying
to make sense of row upon row of hieroglyphics, he often escaped
the cold by slipping into the comfortable temperature of the tea-
tasting room. Thus began his passionate affair with tea. After some
years of hard work, long hours and many opportunities of
handling and tasting tea, snatched at odd moments from his duties
at the dispatch desk, Stuart left Wright, Napier & Co., to work as
sub-agent for a London firm, Joseph Tetley & Co., where he trained
his palate to excellence. In 1871, he set up as a retail dealer at 44
St Enoch Square under the designation 'Stuart Cranston & Co.,
Trained Tea Taster'. He had opted for the retail trade rather than
the wholesale, as dealing with the public suited his eager, intense
nature.

Four years later, well on the way to making Cranston's Teas a
household name using the slogan 'There is no *Tea* like *Cranston's*',
he moved to larger, more central, accommodation at the east
corner of Argyle Street/Queen Street, and there the World's first
'Tea Room' came into being.

To introduce customers to the joys of quality teas, Stuart took to supplying sample cups of new infusions to the ladies who called at his establishment. Unfortunately, this caused some congestion, so he came up with the idea of setting aside a room furnished with tables and chairs purely for tea tasting. This he did, providing accommodation for twelve ladies seated 'elbow to elbow'. After a while, when it dawned on him they were using the room not just for tea tasting but as a meeting place, he had a brilliant flash of inspiration. Why not charge money for their cups of tea? The following announcement appeared in the press:

> A sample cup of 4/- Kaisow, with sugar and cream for 2d — bread and cakes extra; served in the sample room No 2 Queen Street.

No objection to the charge was raised by the ladies. In fact they flocked to Cranstons for tea, cakes and a gossip. The 'Tea Room' had arrived. When it became overcrowded he opened another at 46 Queen Street.

Stuart's next foray into the world of tea came about by chance. One day in 1889, when having a cup of coffee with James McMichael, the Argyll Arcade factor (spelling was flexible when Argyle Street was formed (1760) and the Arcade was built (1828) hence the different versions of Argyll) the conversation turned to the fire in the premises of Copestake, Lindsay, Crampton & Co. on the south side of the Arcade's Buchanan Street arm. Mr McMichael asked Mr Cranston whether he would like to see the ruins. 'Yes, I would' was the reply. His first exclamation on stepping over the debris was, 'I wish I had these premises'. 'Could you fill them?' asked Mr. McMichael. Looking from end to end of the charred and blackened building Stuart replied, 'If I had the chance I would make a very hard try'. 'That's a pity, Mr Cranston', said Mr McMichael, 'but we need not think of it, the old people are coming back'. 'Well, if they don't, let me know', answered Stuart. A few weeks later, Cranston received a letter from James McMichael & Son asking if he wanted to rent the premises. He answered 'yes', that he would turn them into a suite of tea rooms and a dry tea retailing shop. He also acquired the small two-storied building next door, which effectively doubled his floor space and gave him an entrance to his new tea rooms, 26 Buchanan Street. Remodelling complete, his splendid establishment opened on 2 October 1889. The tea rooms, which consisted of a suite of rooms

Advertisement for Cranston's Tea

for ladies only, a general tea room, a gentlemen's tea room and the best ventilated smoking room in the city, were the largest in the world.

All very exciting, but the most novel aspect of the venture was the installation of an early form of air conditioning. According to a full page advertisement in the *Bailie Magazine* (Glasgow's answer to *Punch*), the fresh air, before being admitted to the salons, was cleaned and deprived of all dust or smoke, heated in winter by hot water pipes and cooled in summer by blocks of ice. Air from the rooms was expelled and replaced every 20 minutes by a continuous and imperceptible movement. This innovation stimulated the public's curiosity and people came along in droves to put it to the test. Décor and furnishings were at odds with the ultra-modern ventilation system, being comfortable and traditional.

Cranston opened another tea room at 43 Argyll Arcade in 1892 and a year later added two new departments — Confectionery, where chocolates, marzipans, pastilles, and specialities of all the best French, English and 'Scotch' makers were available and, something completely different, a Japanese Section, with a large, well-chosen stock of oriental knick-knacks. Stuart Cranston was the personification of an entrepreneur. Everything to which he turned his hand was carried out with complete confidence and thoroughness. Tales of his expertise in tea tasting and business abounded — with his assistance — as he believed in self-advertising.

By 1893 Cranston had become the Arcade's largest tenant and the proprietors asked him if he would be interested in owning the whole concern. The idea greatly appealed to the egotistical side of his nature, and immediately he set about raising the necessary finance. Terms of settlement were arranged and the property became his on 28 May 1894. Cranston Tea Rooms Limited were floated in 1896, paving the way in 1898 for Stuart to add to his empire another tea room at 13 Renfield Street. Here again he was asked to take over the whole building, an experience which was repeated bit by bit at his Argyle Street/Queen Street premises until he owned the whole corner block.

A new century dawned and Cranston's Arcade Tea Rooms were bursting at the seams with no room for expansion. His remedy: knock down the old mansion house fronting the premises in Buchanan Street and replace it with a much larger building. Not everyone approved of destroying part of Glasgow's architectural heritage and the *Glasgow Herald* carried an article in 1903, entitled 'The Vanishing Face of Buchanan Street' which stated 'that the building now being demolished, which formed the Buchanan Street entrance to the Argyll Arcade, was, with only one solitary exception, the only link between the past and the present of the

Stuart Cranston.

Street. The building had been to the new city what the Cross Steeple was to the old city — a favourite trysting place for visitors.'

The new, handsome, red-sandstone block designed in French renaissance style by architect Colin Menzies, was more in keeping with Stuart Cranston's grandiose ideas, and provided the Arcade with an imposing frontage — twin archways separated by a central pillar. Each arch was decorated at the top with a colourful mosaic, the left side spelling out the words 'Argyll Arcade' and the right depicting a very grand coat of arms with the date '1904'. The use of the coat of arms was unauthorised and was a typical example of Mr Cranston's pretentiousness. It belonged to the family of Lord Cranstoun, which peerage became extinct in 1869 with the death of Charles Frederick, 11th Lord Cranstoun. Stuart Cranston had no entitlement whatsoever to use it. [This only came to light when I

The new frontage to the Argyll Arcade built by Stuart Cranston.

wrote to the Lord Lyon to find out what the coat of arms depicted, as no-one could enlighten me]. In 1904 Cranston's Tea Rooms Ltd, moved into splendid custom-made tea rooms on the first floor of the new Argyle Arcade Buildings, and instead of entering from 43 Argyle Arcade, customers now climbed a magnificent white marble staircase leading from 28 Buchanan Street. (Now part of Bally shoe shop).

In Edwardian Glasgow, food reform was a current issue and Stuart Cranston came up with the novel idea of opening a fruitarian lunch room in the Arcade which became reality in August 1908. No fewer than 1,000 invitations were issued to regular tea room customers to partake of free luncheons extending over three days. Apart from the health aspect of such a diet, Cranston looked at the venture from a social/economic viewpoint, maintaining that by encouraging the growing of fruits, nuts etc, employment would be created. He reckoned it would take nine men per acre to grow the kindly fruits of the earth, as opposed to one man per acre for the rearing of sheep and cattle. The Fruitarian Room was another success story. The same customers were to be found daily at their favourite tables; indeed, a large number of them had never missed a day since they opened.

Stuart Cranston looked after his staff well. They were under the supervision of a company medical officer and, before legislation required it, they were provided with chairs to rest on when slight pauses occurred in trade (very rarely of course). Behind the scenes Cranston was supported by his lifetime friend and colleague, Robert Cairns, who had worked with him since he had first gone into business. In October 1905, the Limited Company took over from Cranston the three properties he owned — Argyle Arcade, 13 Renfield Street and Argyle/Queen Street corner — so that it carried on its business in premises it owned, thus ensuring security of tenure and revenue from about 100 tenants. The last extension of the business was the taking over of the 'Wellesley' at 145 Sauchiehall Street in 1905. Stuart Cranston retired as managing director of Cranston's Tea Rooms Ltd in 1915, handing over the reins to his right-hand man, Robert Cairns. He died in 1921. His company carried on until the post-war period when bit-by-bit it was sold off. The closing in 1954 of the premises at the corner of Argyle Street/Queen Street was the end of something very special to Glasgow's past and civilisation — Stuart Cranston's little tea room from which grew every other tea room in the world. Cranstons Tea Rooms Limited went into voluntary liquidation in 1955. Like many other similar companies, it didn't survive the tea room's fall from favour. Their linen tablecloths and good china had become old hat: formica-tabled coffee and snack bars had taken their place. However, tea rooms made a welcome comeback as The Guild of Tea Shops' *Guide to the Best Tea Shops in Britain*, published in 1996, proved.

– 13 –
THE BARROWS QUEEN

One of Glasgow's most famous institutions, The Barrows, was started by Maggie McIver, affectionately known as 'The Barrows Queen'. 'Work hard an' keep the heid' was her motto, and it made her a millionaire. Although the epitome of a Glaswegian with her broad Glasgow accent, Maggie was not a native of the city. Her father was a policeman in Galston who transferred to the Glasgow Force, the family first living in Greenhead and then in Bridgeton where Maggie, or Margaret Russell as she was then, attended Boden Street School. Maggie's career as the 'Barrows Queen' started accidentally when a woman hawker at Parkhead Cross asked her to look after her barrow. On her return the woman was astonished to find that the 13-year-old Maggie had not just looked after the barrow, she had started selling from it and was doing a roaring trade. Maggie had enjoyed herself so much that within a year she had her own stall, selling fruit, a trade she augmented by selling oranges round the theatre queues at night. After a while she brought some variety into her business by selling fish in the morning and fruit for the rest of the day. At her regular visits to the Scotch Fruit Bazaar Maggie met a fellow street trader, Samuel McIver, whom she married in 1898. Putting their savings together, the couple started a small fruit business in Bridgeton, bought a pony and float (a two-wheeled cart) and then had a brilliant idea. Why not hire barrows out to those street traders who couldn't afford to buy them? That's exactly what they did, and soon they had over 300 barrows in their yard in Marshall Lane in the Gallowgate. As Mrs McIver told reporter Jack House during an interview in 1954: 'We had over 300 barrahs; all ye could see onywhere ye went was McIver's barrahs. We stertit hirin' them oot at four or five o'clock on a Saturday mornin' an' we used tae hiv tae get the polis tae queue them up. Hirin' a barrah then cost 6d a day — 1s 6d a week. They went up to 2s a day during the war, an 6s a week. Noo it's 6s a day fur a barrah. Makes ye think, eh?'

After the First World War the Corporation Clothes Market in Greendyke Street was demolished, leaving the hawkers without

Maggie McIver 'The Barrows Queen'.

permanent stands, a fate also suffered by the open-air traders at the Old Glasgow Market in Clyde Street, who were evicted, as the ground was needed for building. By then the McIvers were doing very well and, feeling sorry for the displaced traders they bought land in the Calton between Gibson Street and the Gallowgate where they opened a new barrows' market. The venture was a great success and soon the market's reputation had spread far and wide, everything and anything being sold, from fruit, vegetables and fish to clothes, bric-a-brac and even furniture. Maggie had a fondness for furniture, as her mother was a french-polisher who had taught her daughter the tricks of her trade at an early age.

It was not until 1926 that the Barrows, as they were by then known in Glasgow, became a covered market dictated by the Scottish weather, at one point it having rained for six Saturdays in a row. 'Jist think of it', said Maggie, 'the craters are oot hawking fur the stuff. When they get it hame, they take it tae the steamie tae wash the stuff oot an' get it ready for the public. They pit it oot oan the barrah, doon comes the rain, an' it looks like the washin' hingin' oot again!'. Maggie's heart was touched by the plight of the traders and, although many improvised with their own coverings, she decided that the Barrows should have a roof. She therefore had a skeleton building with a roof put up in Moncur Street and replaced the barrows with stalls designed and made by the McIvers. Traders flocked to the new-look Barrows and the biggest market of its kind in Britain was born. The Barrows were open till midnight every Saturday and when the stall-holders started packing up, the McIvers began clearing up. They took the stalls down, stored them away and went round the ground and the adjacent streets sweeping up the leavings and the dirt. There was no law compelling them to do so, but they wanted to be sure that no-one could lay a complaint against the McIvers' Barrows.

After a while Maggie decided to open the Barrows on Sundays as well as Saturdays, the charge for Sunday being two shillings instead of the four shillings charged for a Saturday. It was thought Mrs McIver's Protestant upbringing made her feel there was something sinful in making a profit on the Sabbath. One Sunday Maggie's eldest son, Sam, was sent round collecting rents and had no trouble at all except for a certain large lady known to the McIvers as a 'wide mug'. Every time he approached her she had some excuse for not handing over her two shillings. Eventually in despair he told his mother about it: 'I'll sort her out and you come wi' me Sam.' As soon as the wide mug saw Maggie approaching she got her rent out ready to hand over. Words were exchanged and then the wide mug said 'Ah don't need tae run a stall here, ye know. Ma man's oan the overtime every Sunday, an' he get's double time fur his work.' 'Is that so?', said Mrs McIver. 'Well, if your man can get double time oan a Sunday, so can we.' From the next Sunday the charge for a stall was four shillings instead of two.

At one time Maggie tried opening the Barrows every day of the week but decided it was more bother than it was worth. 'Ye should have seen the electricity bill', she said, clapping her hand to her eyes in horror at the memory of it. 'A' thae lamps oan the stalls, an electric fires forby. Oh ye wouldnae credit it!'.

When Maggie decided to extend the barrows along the Gallowgate, she took over some old buildings and a row of shops which she discovered had belonged to Marion Gilchrist who was murdered in her parlour in West Princes Street on 21 December

The first covered market in Moncur Street.

1908. The buildings were very old and the shops were entered by going up three or four steps. Among them was Tortoloni the cabinet maker, a pawnshop and the Lucky Midden, which was actually part of a sweet factory. The rejected and elderly sweets were thrown out and all the weans along the Gallowgate knew the Lucky Midden. All the old buildings were demolished and Mrs McIver engaged builders to put up the new Barrowland, showing the architect what she wanted by drawing it out on her dining-room table. Before building could start however, a concrete floor had to be laid, a job the McIvers decided to do for themselves, including the preliminary step — digging up the 26,100 square feet area that was to be concreted. On 21 May 1932 James Maxton MP opened the extension to the market which was by then fully enclosed, sides having been added in 1931.

As well as managing an ever-expanding business the McIvers had nine children to care for, and when Maggie's husband died in 1930 from one of his recurring attacks of malaria contracted on his tour of duty during the First World War, he was greatly missed.

Having completed her Barrows complex Maggie's next venture

was to build a function hall above the market. She thought it was a good idea to have a hall attached to the Barrows, as for years she had been organising social functions for the market traders and hawkers, hiring the nearby St Mungo's Halls for the purpose. Maggie laid on a dinner-dance every year and it was the dinner rather than the dance which appealed to her son Sam. 'Soup', he said, 'then a steak pie dinner, a sweet and a cup of tea. Then at 11 o'clock another cup of tea and two cakes in your hand. All for half a dollar (2s.6d). By 1934 The Barrows had its own function suite which Maggie hired out two evenings a week to a dancing master from the South Side. The master brought over a wee band with him and on the very first night the drummer couldn't make it. A 'fill-in' arrived — Billy McGregor, later to become the best known bandleader in Glasgow. The dancing master didn't last long. The East End scared him and he hastened back to the South Side.

When Mrs McIver considered that she charged the dancing master £36 a week but had paid for lighting, heating, taxes and general overheads, she decided to run the place herself. She rented it out to bandleader Billy Blue and his Bluebirds and the famous Barrowland Ballroom was born. It opened on Christmas Eve 1939 with the traders being given a free night. Every stallholder attended, 'done up in aw their finery', the women wearing colourful silk shawls, taffeta dresses and bright jewellery. Billy Blue and the Bluebirds were a great success, and when Maggie saw the huge queues paying to hear them she decided that she could make more profit if she hired her own band and got the dancers' entry money herself. She approached the band's drummer, Billy McGregor, to form a band of his own. He agreed, and Billy McGregor and the Gaybirds emerged.

Like everything else Maggie touched, the Barrowland Ballroom was a gold mine, and by the time the Second World War started it was well established as 'the in place' to be. Couples waltzed, tangoed and foxtrotted the night away until the GI's brought over their jitterbugging and jiving. Such was the fame of the ballroom that it was mentioned in the wartime 'Jairmany Calling' propaganda broadcasts made by Lord Haw Haw, or William Joyce, to give him his real name. He is credited with saying that he knew how well the staff and the girls at Barrowland had treated visiting French, Polish and American soldiers and he hoped that they'd treat the

German victors just as nicely when they marched into Britain! Fortunately, the only casualty of the war in respect of Barrowland was the once famous neon sign on the roof of the ballroom showing a man pushing a barrow. Like all other electric signs it was doused at the beginning of the war, but, although it didn't glow, it was left up and kept in good order. When Lord Haw Haw mentioned the sign in his first broadcast about Barrowland the McIvers were asked to take it down, as it was considered a landmark. By the end of the war jiving had become so popular that a section of the ballroom was cordoned off for jivers, leaving the rest of the hall free for traditional ballroom dancing.

When Maggie was running the Barrows and bringing up her family she went out dancing every night in the week. On Fridays she was out till 3 a.m. Even in her seventies, with her 'bad foot' (to quote her), she could be so bewitched by Billy McGregor's music that she often took the floor.

Although the ballroom burned down in 1958, Glasgow had not seen the end of it, for it reopened with great ceremony on Christmas Eve 1960, sporting a magnificent new neon sign. Over the years most of the great bandleaders of their time, Joe Loss, Henry Hall, Ray Fox, Jack Hilton, played at Barrowland. Stars such as Johnny Dankworth and Cleo Laine appeared and singer Lena Martell was once resident vocalist. Today it is a venue for stars and top groups.

The Barrows was not only a marketplace; it was a place of entertainment. People flocked to enjoy the patter and antics of some traders, like the negro wearing a white turban who went by the name of 'Chief Adobou' and claimed that his snake oil would cure a myriad of complaints from callouses to baldness, and 'Irish Paddy' the strongman who miraculously escaped from yards of thick chains and half a dozen padlocks. The following story about Paddy casts doubt on the authenticity of his escapes. He was said to have arranged to be 'padlocked' by friends using his specially designed locks, but one day, after a minor dispute, his friends chained him up using conventional padlocks and then left him to his own devices. Paddy's reputation was not enhanced when the Fire Brigade had to come and saw his padlocks off. His strength was not in doubt however. He performed tremendous feats of strength and endurance, inviting the public to smash giant sandstone blocks on his chest with a sledgehammer, balancing cartwheels and eating shoals of live goldfish while piercing his cheeks with six inch needles!

There were stalls selling clothes, food, sweeties, books, flowers, records, comics, toys and even one that did 'cut-price printing'. On the whole however, the stallholders were silent people. For the fun you had to go to the main concourse where traders, grafters, as they were called, sold from the back of vans. They were the ones with the sharpwitted banter that delighted Glaswegians. Many were East End Londoners like 'Cockney Jock' who bombarded his audience with incredible stores of 'southsea island pearls' for thirty bob (£1.50). Grafters could make you believe they were giving their goods away for almost nothing. They started their *spiel* with a ridiculously high price, working their way down to what they were looking for in the first place, by which time everyone in the audience thought they were getting the bargain of a lifetime. 'I'm not asking a tenner, I wouldn't even take a fiver, madam. Would you give me two quid for this magnificent piece of craftmanship? Yes? Well, I don't want two quid, not even thirty bob. I'm practically giving them away today for 15 shillings. This final knockdown price was delivered with a crescendo and a momentous clap of the grafter's hands. By then the public couldn't wait to get their hands on the bargain and pushed and shoved to the front of the crowd to make sure they were not disappointed. A day out at the Barrows became a regular weekly outing for thousands of families. People came in coachloads from all over Scotland to listen to the patter of the showmen and auctioneers — and, of course, to get a bargain.

Despite being a millionaire, at the age of 75 Maggie McIver was still working a seven-day week from nine in the morning to six at night in her draughty secondhand furniture shop straight across from the Barrows. She said that she had opened the shop for her daughter, but the real reason was that she couldn't bear to retire. As she always said: 'Work hard an' keep the heid.' When Maggie wasn't french polishing some of the furniture in the shop she sat in an old armchair at the back of it, dressed in a navy blue coat and black toque hat. However, when her daughter and assistant attended to customers who were lingering uncertainly at the open doorway she would shout out: 'Choice chips an' rare bits! Is that man wantin gramyphone records eh? There are merr records up here if ye want some!'. For all her wealth Maggie was always a woman of the Gallowgate and always spoke with a good old 'Brigton' tongue. Maggie McIver died in 1958, the same year her ballroom burned down. It was the end of an era and a remarkable woman. She had come to Glasgow from Galston when she was seven years old and had made her fortune through hard work, determination and an amazingly astute business mind. That she had also managed to bring up nine children at the same time made her all the more remarkable.

– 14 –
A MAN AHEAD OF HIS TIME

Transport systems of the future look certain to include monorails. However, as far back as 1930 inventor George Bennie launched his railplane which he was convinced was the key to the future — a new era in travel. When hundreds of people flocked to Milngavie on the outskirts of Glasgow to witness the launch on 8 July 1930, they couldn't believe their eyes, for there, in a field built over a length of ordinary railway line, was a sturdy framework of steel girders, a tiny station 30 feet above the earth and, most amazing of all, a white, cigar-shaped carriage with propellers at each end. Officials, guests and the press climbed the steps to the fairylike station, and flashbulbs popped when electrically-powered propellers accelerated the 10-tonne carriage smoothly along the 426 feet of track. With fifty passengers on board the Bennie Railplane had made its first run.

The son of an engineer, George Bennie was born in Auldhouse in 1892. His love of tinkering and passion for trains led him into the field of design, and it was while working on plans for diesel engines that he first conceived his railplane. Almost from the start the brilliant idea received wide acclaim, winning him a gold medal at the 1922 Industrial Exhibition in Edinburgh. Convinced that a fortune was within his grasp, he ploughed every penny into setting up a test track, though it was several years before he could raise backing to turn his dream into reality.

The brochure advertising the launch of the George Bennie Railplane System of Transport, to give it its full title, said it had been originated and developed to a practical conclusion and would be a universal means of transport by land, by virtue of the following factors:

1. The insistent demand for safe and rapid transport.
2. A new method of transport is urgently required in industrial centres due to the present congestion of roads.
3. A cheap method of transport is urgently required for the development of rural districts for the transport of mails, perishable goods, etc., and for the opening of new and undeveloped countries.

The brochure went on to point out:

There is a fourth factor, one of great importance, and this may best be explained by stating the now obvious fact that fast passenger traffic should be completely separated from slow or heavy goods traffic.

By building the George Bennie Railplane System of Transport over the existing railways and making it a fast passenger, mails and perishable goods service, most of the revenue lost to the railways will flow back.

Our railways are a national asset. They cannot be allowed to go under in the transport competition. It is intended that the George Bennie Railplane System of Transport will restore them to their lost economic position by acting as a feeder to the main line, and also relieve them of the congestion of passengers and goods. The railplane will take all passenger traffic, and thereby relieve the railways absolutely for high-speed goods traffic. Another important aspect of this is that when the existing railways will carry only goods traffic, no night work will be necessary, with a resultant saving of at least 60% of operating costs to the railway companies.

The brochure went on to describe the mechanics of the system, which appeared to be that the passenger car was self-propelled, driven by air-screws fore and aft, suspended from above — not, like a railway coach, resting on wheels below. Inside it was luxurious. The door, with its tasteful stained-glass oval window, slid noiselessly back to reveal a thick carpet, and on each side the most comfortable easy chairs imaginable. Table lamps were placed on semicircular ledges between the chairs, there was electric light and the windows were curtained. The railplane was not like a train or a road-coach, it was like a home or an exclusive club. In the driver's cabin everything was built for safety. There was a powerful electric motor to drive the shaft that rotated the propellers and a window in the nose of the car gave the driver a clear view of his track. The double braking system was so cleverly designed that should there be danger ahead the brakes were automatically applied — a very reassuring feature when travelling at 120 miles per hour. As the weight of the car and passengers ensured stability, the railplane could not jump its rails. Nor could it sway from side to side, passengers only noticing it was moving by gazing out of the window and watching the countryside rapidly fly past. On comparing a railway with a railplane, the railplane came out on top. It could be erected over existing railway tracks, could cross roads and streams or go up small hills where a railway would need

George Bennie's cigar shaped railplane.

bridges and tunnels, both costly things. It could also travel at more than double the speed of a passenger train with less wear and tear and much more cheaply. It was hoped to accomplish the journey between Glasgow and Edinburgh in just twenty minutes, speeds of 150 miles per hour being anticipated.

The Bennie Railplane System of Transport also won hands down over other forms of transport when it came to construction costs. To lay a double railway track cost from £45,000 to £60,000 per mile, a double tramway track from £25,000 to £30,000 a mile, and the tubes in London, laboriously tunnelled through clay, gravel and rock £80,000 per mile. To lay a double track for the railplane cost £19,000 per mile, so if a new line was to be laid, double track, to join two towns twenty miles apart it would cost £820,000 less than an ordinary railway line. For George Bennie the launch of his railplane was the realisation of a dream. He felt it was the beginning of something big, and as the interest was immense, he quickly tried to capitalise, travelling the world to promote his brainchild. However, despite massive interest, the economic climate and opposition from the big railway companies combined to crush his dream and the railplane was left to rust in its field at Milngavie, leaving Bennie a sad, disillusioned man.

George Primrose, a retired accountant, contacted Bennie in the 1940s after finding some of his designs in an old box. 'When I met

The luxurious inside of the railplane.

Bennie' he said, 'he was running a herbalist shop. He was a terrifically dynamic man, but seeing his old plans hit him hard. Somehow you couldn't help feeling sorry for him.' There were neither press nor crowds around when the rusting hulk of the Bennie Railplane was dismantled and carted off for scrap in 1956.

A year later Bennie died bankrupt and unknown, and today all that's left of his pioneering concept is a small plaque on the site where his railplane once stood. But, who knows, perhaps one day rivers will be spanned by railplane and bridges and roads will have pylons carrying a network of tracks from town to town across them. Perhaps we shall half-ride and half-fly above the earth in a railplane. It certainly would solve a lot of today's transport problems and would be a wonderful memorial to George Bennie — a man ahead of his time.

– 15 –
WEST OF SCOTLAND CRICKET CLUB, PARTICK

This article has nothing to do with cricket. Then why head it up West of Scotland Cricket Club, Partick, I can hear you say? Well, it's because the world's first international football match was held there on 30 November 1872. This match was the first official football match played between two countries, although previously there had been three unofficial matches in London. These had been arranged by the Secretary of the Football Association, Charles Alcock, who wrote to the *Glasgow Herald* expressing a wish to organise matches between Scottish and English players. Alcock selected both sides and the qualification for the Scottish one seems to have been largely a matter of evening up the sides with the 'English' team, one player qualifying for Scotland because he used to enjoy shooting there. The Scottish teams, made up of Anglo-Scots, failed to win any of the games. The 'Alcock Internationals' as they were called had no official standing, and it was in 1872 that international football really began when a truly Scottish team took the field against an English international team. Thus began the world's first international football game and the first clash between Scotland and England which became a yearly fixture unequalled anywhere in the world because of the intense rivalry between the two sides.

As already mentioned the game took place at the West of Scotland Cricket Ground, Hamilton Crescent, Partick, and because of their pre-eminence in Scottish football, Queen's Park not only arranged it but provided all the players for the Scottish side: Robert Gardner, William Ker, James Taylor, J.J. Thomson, James Smith, Robert Smith, Robert Leckie, Alex Rhind, W. McKinnon, J.B. Weir and D. Wotherspoon. The formation of the team was listed as 2:2:6. Admission was one shilling and the ticket stated that the game would be played by Association Rules, which meant English Association Rules, as then there was no Scottish Football Association. (It didn't come until 1873). Four thousand people attended the game and gate receipts were reported as £102 19s 6d, resulting in a profit of £33 for Queens Park.

If television had been around in 1872 and the first international had been filmed, the game would bear no relation to that of today. Free kicks were a few years away and there was vagueness about what happened when the ball went out of play, the English preferring to throw it back with one hand and the Scots with two. As whistles did not appear on the field until 1878 the referee waved a handkerchief about furiously to stop and start the game, and as there were no penalty kicks until 1891, infringements around the goals went unpunished. (Incidentally, crossbars didn't come until 1875). Even the players' kit would look alien today. They wore heavy woollen jerseys without numbers on the back (identification came from their variously coloured striped socks) and funny little hats called cauls, which looked like Wee Willie Winkie's night cap. The jerseys were blue — Queen's Park's original colours — as they didn't adopt their famous black and white hoops until 1874. Boots were built for power rather than skill, and as removable studs only arrived in the 1880s an individual boot could weigh more than one-and-a-quarter pounds. Footballs were also heavy, cumbersome and hand-laced, making them unpredictable in performance when wet and muddy.

The result of the game was a goal-less draw, but it was said that Scotland deserved to win it. Sounds familiar doesn't it? A goal-less draw it may have ended, but the correspondent of *Bell's Life in London* reported: 'A splendid display of football in the really scientific sense of the word, and a most determined effort on the part of the representatives of the two nationalities to overcome one another.' The Scots suffered a 4-2 defeat at Kennington Oval in London the following year, but in 1874 it was their turn to win, with a score of 2-1, and a brilliant midfielder called McNeil was carried off the field shoulder high in triumph. Lack of rules in those informal days was beneficial to some players, like Scottish defender, Arthur Kinnaird, known as a bit of a 'hacker' or 'if you can't get the ball, get the man' type of player. Apparently, because he was concerned about the Scot's lack of discipline, Sir Francis Mandarin, President of the English FA, visited Kinnaird's mother's house and when she said to him, 'You know, I'm afraid that one day Arthur will come home with a broken leg' replied, ' I shouldn't worry about that ma'am if I were you. It won't be his own!'. When the English captain asked Kinnaird before the game began, 'Shall we play fair or shall we have hacking?', Kinnaird was said to have replied, 'Oh, let's have hacking.'!

Because of a dispute between the photographer and the players, there are few souvenirs of the first international. It seems that the players would not promise to buy prints from the photographer and the English ridiculed him by pulling faces. Fortunately, however, The Scottish Football Association Museum Trust hold in their collection a match ticket, a cap worn by a Scottish player and the only images in existence of the game — drawings taken from the *Daily Graphic* newspaper. There were a number of repercussions as a result of the game. First, the organisation of football in Scotland was placed on a more established footing and there was a surge of interest in football, with new clubs being formed, including Dumbarton and Glasgow Rangers. It then became clear that a central body was required to organise the Scottish game, and in 1873 Queens Park invited the other leading Scottish clubs to a meeting to establish a Challenge Cup and a Scottish Football Association to promote the game and settle disputes between member clubs. The clubs whose representatives attended the meeting were: Queen's Park, Clydesdale, Vale of Leven, Dumbreck, Third Lanark Rifle Volunteer Reserves, Eastern, Granville and Rovers. At the end of the meeting it had been agreed that each club would donate £1 towards the purchase of a trophy to be known as the Scottish Cup, which would be competed for annually. Sixteen clubs entered the inaugural competition in 1874 and in the final Queen's Park beat Clydesdale 2-0, heralding a three-year run of straight victories. Changes also came on the field, with football taking on a more scientific and tactical aspect. The tactics the Scots used impressed the English, whose game was based around dribbling that relied on the individual sporting prowess of its players. In contrast, Scotland played a passing game that emphasised support for the player in possession, a philosophy around which all subsequent tactical innovations was woven.

From that first international game came the inspiration for the development of the international series, and Scotland v. England matches became the focus for national pride from then on. Scotland, with their edge in tactical innovation enjoyed much of the early success, and records and heroes were soon established.

GLASGOW CURIOSITIES

The first star player for Scotland was the famous Walter Arnott, who as a boy had watched the first international by standing on a cab and looking over the wall. He became hooked on football and later joined Queens Park and played for Scotland against England ten times in succession between 1884 and 1893.

Now that you have read all this, if anybody mentions the West of Scotland Cricket Ground, you will know they are not expecting a conversation about cricket; it will be about football and the greatest fixture in the world, Scotland v. England, suspended in the 1980s because of the hooligan behaviour of the fans. Let's hope that one day it will be possible to play it again when the fans on both sides learn how to behave and can leave their xenophobic attitude at home and not take it to the football ground.

– 16 –
GLASGOW'S OWN DOGE'S PALACE

Even among Venice's many architectural gems, the Doge's Palace is exceptional and essential on the itinerary of tourists visiting the city. However, what those tourists don't know is that Glasgow also has a Doge's Palace. It's the former Templeton carpet factory facing Glasgow Green, and while not nearly as old as its Venetian namesake, how Glasgow came to have it is an interesting, albeit tragic story.

James Templeton started his chenille carpet-making business in the early 1840s. His first factory was in King Street, Calton, and when that burned down on Christmas Day 1856 he took over McPhail's Cotton Mill in William Street (renamed Templeton Street). The company went from strength to strength until it was a household name worldwide and, in 1887, on securing the sole patent rights (excepting America) to manufacture Spool Axminster carpets by a new process, ordered thirty new looms and earmarked the west side of the Templeton Street site for a new factory to house them. Despite John Stewart Templeton, James's son, engaging a leading architect of the day, Helensburgh-born William Leiper, to design his new factory, the plans proved to be somewhat of a problem. One by one, three different sets were drawn up and rejected by the city fathers as unsuitable, because it was said, as the proposed new building was to face Glasgow Green, the city's principal park, they didn't want a common factory defacing it; they wanted something to enhance it. Finally, in exasperation and desperation, Templeton asked Leiper what he considered to be the finest building in the world. 'The Doge's Palace' he replied. 'Then design our new building like that', said Templeton. Leiper did. He submitted his plans which, wonder upon wonder, were approved, and permission was granted to go ahead with the exotically designed Albert Mills.

Work on the new factory began in September 1888 and thereafter progressed according to plan, that is, until 1 November 1889, when it became the scene of an appalling tragedy. It happened at 5.15 p.m. when the builders had left work and a severe gale was blowing from the north-west. Three powerful gusts of wind in rapid succession caught the partially built west wall, causing it to collapse with a sound like thunder through the roof of the adjoining weaving shed where 140 women and 4 men were employed. About 900 people worked in the factory altogether, and no sooner had the gable fallen than everyone panicked (not only those in the weaving shed) as every department shook as if an earthquake had occurred. Those in the weaving shed uninjured by the falling mass of masonry fled, terror-stricken, towards the main door in William Street. At least 70 girls escaped in that way, but many others bravely remained by the side of their less fortunate workmates and helped them from the shed. The ill-fated single-storey weaving shed was in fact the cotton mill taken over by Templetons in 1856, and the new building was being constructed around it. 'There was no doubt about the timing of the collapse', said one newspaper, 'for the clock in the weaving shed still stands with its hands pointing to the fatal moment.' Even before the fire brigade, salvage corps, ambulances and police arrived, despite the winter darkness, rescuers were frantically digging out those buried. Later the captain of the fire brigade said that he thought he had been called to a fire, but instead 'came to a scene of utter darkness and dismay.' A Mr Stewart, whose home overlooked the mill, was sitting writing when he heard the dreadful crash, followed by the screams and groans of the injured mill girls. Understanding what had happened and knowing the district well, he immediately rushed to the police station.

One way of describing what happened that dreadful night is to repeat the words of Ex-Bailie Waddel, one of the first on the scene after the disaster:

I was sitting in my house in Monteith Row when the accident happened. The wind was very high and was coming in fierce gusts. Suddenly I heard a sound like thunder and ran out to see what had happened. On looking towards the mill, I saw that the walls had collapsed. I made my way there and found the courtyard filled with workers. Many of the girls were hysterical. I then made my way to the weaving shed. The whole place was in darkness but a rescue party had been organised and was relieving from among the debris as many of the imprisoned workers as it could reach. A workroom had been set aside for receiving the injured who were attended by the medical men who had arrived. The Fire Brigade and Salvage Corps arrived simultaneously with myself, and lent every assistance in the rescue work. Lamps and lanterns were at first used, but very quickly electric light was introduced and assisted materially in the work.

Throughout the night rescuers painstakingly searched through the debris until it was certain that all the bodies had been recovered. In all 29 women died and 20 were injured. The first corpse to be brought out was that of 20-year-old Jeannie Glass, and her battered body was the forerunner of many of her work-mates, one of whom was only 13. Luckily, others had miraculous escapes, like Margaret McCulloch who was buried in the ruins for an hour and a half before being rescued:

I was working near the wooden partition dividing the shed from the new mill, and about five o'clock decided to clean up my loom. The first thing I heard was a strange rumbling noise and I thought the boilers had burst. Then came the crash and suddenly all became dark. I was struck on the head, but didn't know what with. My legs and arms were bruised. I was doubled up, my head being forced down to my knees. Although I was injured and terrified and had no idea what had happened, I never lost my senses and kept shouting for help. After a while I heard the men working above me and eventually one put a stick through a hole and asked me to take hold of it to see how far down I was. I grasped the stick and the men kept calling to me to 'cheer up lassie, we'll be sure to get you out', which helped me to keep up my heart. I was getting very weak and faint, but soon the men got a hole above me and handed through a drink of water which recovered me greatly and in a little while I was got out.

Shearer, the man who was in charge of the looms, was another lucky worker. At 5.14 he had left his office to go and check on one of the boilers. At 5.15 his office disappeared under rubble. Afterwards he said he would remember forever the pitiful cries for help coming through the darkness. One woman had a premonition that something was about to happen. Robina Boyle told her rescuers that her mate at the next loom, Maggie Lindsay, had turned to her minutes before the crash saying 'Oh Beenie, I'm feart. I think something's gaun tae happen.'

When Queen Victoria heard of the tragedy she had a message sent to Sir James King, Glasgow's Lord Provost: 'The Queen asks for further news in respect of the catastrophe at Templetons Mills and commands me to express her sincere sympathy with the sufferers,' to which the Lord Provost replied: 'The Lord Provost

Glasgow's Doge's Palace.

heartily thanks her Majesty for the gracious message of sympathy. The total deaths are twenty-nine and he has personally visited this morning the nine sufferers in the Royal Infirmary and on the whole they are progressing favourably.'

As the initial shock abated, attention turned to the cause of the tragedy. Ex-Bailie Waddel believed that when the wind caught the heavy crane placed on the top of the building, the crane fell, carrying the whole building along with it. The *Glasgow Herald* leader column however, deplored the lack of adequate security and posed a rather surprising hypothesis, 'Was it an accident? Should 140 women have been allowed to toil day after day with such a huge unstable pile hanging over them?'. As the press elaborated on that theme the search for a scapegoat inevitably fell on William Leiper. Allegations were made about 'strange defects in the construction' and his exotically designed building was described as 'an architectural absurdity', 'a preposterous joke' and 'an epic folly'. One report suggesting that the building's foundations had been weakened by mining earlier, was dismissed as nonsense by the site surveyor.

However, all the speculation had to wait for the official enquiry on Friday 20 December at which Mr T.L. Watson, a leading architect, ridiculed the accusations of 'strange defects in the construction'. 'The building has been regularly monitored' he said, and in his opinion everyone concerned with it had been thorough and professional in every respect. Statements from other architects agreed, and accusations levelled by the press were dismissed as being clever after the event. There was a long debate on who was responsible for the construction of the building — Alexander Harvey, the site engineer, or William Leiper. It was no secret that Harvey disliked Leiper intensely, and many said his animosity was the main cause of the collapse, as for some reason or other, he saw fit to omit the stabilising floors as the building progressed. However, on being questioned by Mr W.W. Robertson, one of the commissioners appointed to chair the enquiry, Leiper explained that he was only responsible for designing the elevations:

Leiper: Perhaps I may be allowed to state my position exactly. Plans were brought to me by Mr Templeton of a building already designed by engineers and mill architects. Everything was fixed, the height and thickness of the walls, length and mode of flooring and roofing. My commission was to design elevations and outside ornamentation, the engineers undertaking the design structure portions and all the iron work, floors, roofs etc. I designed the elevations incorporating the original plans. The understanding with Mr Templeton was that I would have nothing to do with the structural portions internally. It is a matter on which I was never consulted and I do not profess to be a mill architect.

Robertson: Your statement differs from that of Mr Templeton's in one very important particular. He said that he asked you to arrange the plans and the general arrangement of the mill with a view to its fitness in carrying on the special work for which it was intended. You say Mr Harvey was the engineer to the whole structure, that he was the person employed to design it and your function was to bring it into architecturally satisfactory form.'

Leiper: Yes, that is my position.

Robertson: But that is not what we heard from Mr Templeton.

Leiper: That is my point exactly.

Robertson: I suppose there is nothing in writing on the subject, was this all arranged by verbal communication?

Leiper: It was.

Robertson: You see the importance of the distinction.

Leiper: Well, I have the drawings which are as good as writing and which were put into my hands. They were not merely sketch plans, but a complete tracing given to me by Mr Templeton. I knew nothing about looms but Mr Templeton said he was arranging that with Mr Harvey who was in the habit of designing mills. He arranged with Mr Harvey that I do the elevations and he was to do that portion which was distinctly the work of a mill architect. All the iron work was made from drawings that I never saw until they were afterwards put in the hands of the founder.

There then came a lengthy discussion on the nature and effect of the gale on the fateful night, and despite Sir William Arrol differing sharply with Professor Grant of Glasgow Observatory, both gave it as their opinion that William Leiper had followed correct construction procedures and was in no way to blame for what had happened. The result of the enquiry was that no-one was to blame — hard to believe, as it was accepted that a 70-feet-high wall with mortar still fresh, without cross walls and roof, was obviously vulnerable, and had the upper floors been in place there would have been no collapse.

Reconstruction commenced after the enquiry, and early in 1892 Leiper's magnificent building was completed. Glasgow at last had her Doge's Palace, replicated in terra-cotta, red brick, deep blue, gold and white mosiac, and at the topmost storey, red and green glazed bricks zigzagged against a bright yellow ground. It proudly faced Glasgow Green in all its Moorish-Italian splendour and remains to this day an outstanding feature of the Glasgow landscape and a monument to the young lives lost.

– 17 –
SOME WEE STORIES FROM THE ARCHIVES

John Smith, Bookseller, Glasgow, and Burns the Poet

When Robert Burns published the Edinburgh edition of his poems in 1787, he asked John Smith, the founder of Scotland's oldest firm of booksellers, John Smith & Sons (1751) to distribute copies to subscribers in and around Glasgow. However, on squaring up with Mr Smith for doing so, Burns, astonished to find that Mr Smith would only accept five per cent commission for his trouble, commented: 'Ye seem to be a very decent sort o' folk, you Glasgow booksellers, but oh, they're sair birkies in Edinburgh.'

Dr James Jeffrey's Ghastly Galvanic Experiment

At Glasgow Circuit Court in October 1819, collier Matthew Clydesdale was condemned to death for murder. On passing sentence the judge, as was the custom, ordered that after the execution the body should be given to Dr James Jeffrey, the lecturer on anatomy in the University, 'to be publicly dissected and anatomised'.

After the execution on 4 November the body was taken to the college dissecting theatre, where students and members of the public gathered to witness an experiment on it with the newly invented galvanic battery. The corpse was placed in a sitting position in a chair and light air tubes connected to the battery were inserted in its nostrils. What happened next was like a scene from a horror movie, for hardly had the battery been set working than the chest of the dead man heaved, his eyes opened widely, staring apparently in astonishment around him; his head, arms and legs moved, and he attempted to rise to his feet. Although some of the audience screamed out in horror and some fainted, others cheered at what they believed to be a triumph of science. However, so amazed and alarmed was Dr Jeffrey that he plunged a knife into the jugular vein of the murderer, who instantly fell down on the floor.

For a long time the community discussed whether Clydesdale had really been dead when the battery was applied, or whether it had been a miracle of science. However, the most logical conclusion had to be that he had not been dead, easily explained by death on the scaffold being slow in those days. With no long drop to break the spinal cord, it was simply a case of strangulation, and obviously Clydesdale's neck had not been dislocated. After those gruesome happenings there was never another case of dissection under sentence of the Courts in Glasgow University.

The Bewitched Baronet

At the end of the 17th century, Sir George Maxwell of Pollok's severe and mysterious illness, for which the doctors could do nothing, was put down to witchcraft. Having heard of the speculation a young servant woman undertook to discover the offenders. She immediately set about her investigations, and to the astonishment of all she accused several of the most respectable tenants on the Pollok estate. However, what no-one knew was that these were all people against whom she had vendettas and she had cunningly hidden clay images stuck full of pins about their houses, afterwards pretending to have found them, thus giving credibility to her foul accusations.

The Government ordered a special commission to investigate the matter, and the charges were found to be clearly proven. As a coinsequence, at least seven people were sentenced to be strangled and burned — a sentence which, however monstrous it may now appear, was rigidly carried out.

Mrs Hare Lynched in Glasgow and Rescued by the Police

On Tuesday 10 February, 1829, the *Glasgow Chronicle* announced that, on that day, Mrs Hare, wife of Burke's associate member, had been rescued by the police from the fury of a Glasgow mob. She had travelled on foot from Edinburgh with her infant daughter in her arms — a weary, miserable journey, trying to avoid discovery and often sleeping by roadsides and in hay-ricks.

The *Chronicle* stated that the Glasgow Calton Police had to lodge her in a cell to save her and her child from infuriated citizens. Her story was that she had been lodging in the Calton for four nights 'with her infant and her bit duds' and that the people with whom she stayed were unaware of her identity. She said that she hoped to leave Glasgow without detection and had kept to the house during the day, only venturing out occasionally in the early morning or twilight to the Broomielaw to find out when a vessel would be sailing for Ireland. On the morning of the 10th she had gone out with the same objective but, on her way back to her lodgings by way of Clyde Street she was recognised by a drunken woman who shouted out 'Hare's wife — burke her', and, picking up a large stone, threw it at her. The large crowd that rapidly gathered followed the woman's example and set about Mrs Hare, who fortunately managed to escape from her persecutors and fled into Calton. She was not out of danger however. The unfortunate woman was pursued there and was experiencing very rough treatment when the police rescued her.

Because of the attitude of the public, the authorities realised that they themselves had to get Mrs Hare safely on her way to Ireland. However, on the afternoon of her rescue an immense crowd surrounded the police office expecting to see her depart. Fearing another riot, she was detained in custody until Thursday 12 February when she sailed from the Broomielaw in the steamer *Fingal* bound for Belfast. While the *Fingal* lay at Greenock to take on cargo, Mrs Hare remained under the guardianship of the local police, and few were ever aware that she had been anywhere near that town..

Prince Charles Edward Stuart and Miss Clementina Walkinshaw

When Prince Charles Edward Stuart was in Glasgow in 1745/46 he was said to have done his utmost to ingratiate himself with the citizens. Dressed in fine silk tartan with crimson velvet breeches he ate twice a day in one of the front rooms of the finest house in the city, the Shawfield Mansion, in which he had taken up residence.

All his charm and manners however, had little effect upon the people of Glasgow. He got got nowhere with the ladies and as for the men, Provost Cochrane related that the only recruit he got was 'Ane drunken shoemaker, who must have fled his country for debt, if he had not for treason.' When the prince left the city on 3 January 1746 after a stay of ten days, he said he admired the beauty and regularity with which it was built, but nowhere had he found so few friends. There was however, one notable exception, for it was while he was in Glasgow that he met Clementina Walkinshaw, who after his escape to France was sent for by him and became his mistress. Clementina was the youngest daughter of John

Walkinshaw of Camlachie and Barrowfield and was said to have been a very beautiful woman. She was later created Countess Alberstorff by the King of France. The Prince and Clementina had a daughter, Charlotte, in 1754. However, it was not until 1787 that she was legitimised by a special deed recorded in the parliamentary register of Paris, when she became Charlotte Stuart, Duchess of Albany.

Clementina died at a good old age in 1802, fourteen years after her royal lover who died in Rome in 1788 aged 67. Their relationship had only lasted eight years, and in his last days it was his daughter Charlotte who nursed him while her mother Clementina brought up her children. Shortly after her father's death, Charlotte contracted a fatal disease and died whilst in Rome sorting out her father's estate.

The First Glasgow Umbrella

In 1782 a Dr Jamieson was the first person to introduce an umbrella to Glasgow. He had brought it from Paris, and when he began unfurling it on the streets, crowds of people followed him in amazement. It was four years before anyone was enterprising enough to attempt to manufacture umbrellas in the city, and the person who did so was John Gardner. However, he was not very successful. 'I have had in my hands' wrote Senex, a famous historian of the time, 'the first umbrella that was ever made in Glasgow. It was indeed a very clumsy article. The cloth was heavy oil or wax-glazed linen, and the ribs were formed of Indian cane, such as shortly before this time ladies were accustomed to use as hoops to extend their petticoats. The handle was massy and strong, and altogether it was a load to carry.'

Unfortunately, Mr Gardner was obliged to give up his manufacture, as a Manchester firm had been able to make a lighter article at a cheaper price. But John Gardner was not a man to give up easily, and his next attempt to be innovative was to manufacture pianofortes which were then coming into fashion in Glasgow, displacing the old spinets. Again he had no luck. His first instrument was so defective in some of its parts that he did not even complete it. Anyway, the importation of highly finished pianofortes from London made him despair of being able to compete successfully.

Glasgow Minister's Turn to Tak' a Scunner

This little tale is reproduced exactly as it was written in *Anecdotage of Glasgow*, by Robert Alison, printed in 1892:

Once upon a time, as the prelude to old stories used to run, a pair of human turtles made their appearance before a Glasgow minister and desired to be united in the bonds of sacred wedlock. Finding the preliminaries all satisfactory, the minister proceeded with the ceremony till he came to that part of it where the question is put to the bridegroom: 'Are you willing to take this woman to be your lawful wedded wife?' To this necessary query the man, after some considerable hesitation, answered: 'No.'

'No!', said the minister, with a look of surprise, 'for what reason?'

'Just', said the poor, embarrassed simpleton, looking round for the door, 'because I've ta'en a scunner [disgust] at her.'

On this, the ceremony, to the evident mortification of the fair one, was broken off, and the parties retired. A few days after, however, they again presented themselves before his reverence, and the fastidious bridegroom, having declared that he had got over his objections, the ceremony was again commenced, and proceeded without interruption until the question was put to the bride: 'Are you willing to take this man to be your lawful wedded husband?' To which she answered: 'No!' 'What is the meaning of this?' said the minister, evidently displeased at the fickle folly of the pair, and their silly trifling in a matter of such serious importance. 'Oh, naething at all,' said the blushing damsel, tossing her head with an air of resentment, 'only, I've just ta'en a scunner at him.'

The two again retired to their lonely pillows; and lonely indeed it would seem they had found them, for the reverend gentleman, on coming out of his house the following morning, met the foolish couple once more on their way to solicit his services.

'It's a' made up noo,' said the smiling fair one. 'Oh yes,' said her intended. 'It's a' settled noo, and we want ye to marry us as soon as possible.' 'I will do no such thing' was the grave and startling reply of the minister to this impatient request. 'What for?' cried the fickle pair, speaking together in a tone of mingled surprise and disappointment. 'Oh, naething at all,' said his reverence, passing on his way, 'but I've just ta'en a scunner at ye baith.'

– 18 –
THE STATUE WITH THE MOVING TAIL

The story of the statue with the moving tail is a romantic one. However, to tell it we have to go back to the early 18th century when Glasgow got its very first statue, King William of Orange on horseback, better known to Glaswegians as 'King Billy'. That he looks more like Julius Caesar has often been commented on, but it appears that it was the fashion at the time to portray eminent men as Roman emperors. King Billy was a gift to the city from James MacRae, a poor washerwoman's son from Ayr who left home at an early age, and after finding employment with the East India Company worked his way up until eventually he became Governor of Madras.

When, laden with honours and wealth, Governor MacRae returned to Ayr nearly half a century after he had left it, few recognised in the distinguished stranger the boy who had gone to sea so long ago. On beginning to look for relatives MacRae discovered that his mother had been cared for in her last days by a niece, Bell, and her husband, itinerant fiddler Hugh McGuire, and to repay their kindness, MacRae provided for their four daughters by showering money, education and clothes on them. The eldest Lizzie, (or Leezie) was married to the Earl of Glencairn and on her wedding day she received from MacRae the estate of Ochiltree and diamonds worth £45,000. The second got an estate and married James Erskine, afterwards Lord Alva. The third married Governor MacRae's 'nephew' (otherwise his illegitimate son) and received an estate in Dumfriesshire. The fourth, the old man's favourite, married Charles Dalrymple and received the estate of Orangefield in Ayrshire.

It was in 1734, two years after coming home, that Governor MacRae presented the statue of King Billy to Glasgow, of which he was then a burgess. Whether at the time the citizens were pleased to have a statue of King Billy foisted on them, we don't know, but later it became a sort of religious totem pole between Protestants and Roman Catholics. King Billy, for those who don't know, fought and defeated King James II of England and VII of

The statue of King Billy at Cathedral Square, showing the mobile tail.

Scotland at the Battle of the Boyne in 1690, an event still celebrated in Glasgow by those who continue to see Catholicism as a threat.

As to why MacRae chose King Billy for Glasgow's first statue, it was suggested that during his boyhood in Ayr he had probably seen something and heard a great deal of the cruel deeds of the persecuting times of Charles II and James VII and II and had put up the statue as a token of regard for the king who had ended those evil days. What Prince Charles Edward Stuart must have thought of it when he arrived in Glasgow on Christmas Day in 1745 at the head of his ragged and worn-out army is not hard to imagine. It certainly would not have given him confidence that the people of Glasgow would be on his side.

At first the controversial statue stood by the pavement in front of the Tolbooth at the Cross. It was then moved along the newly widened Trongate towards Argyle Street and placed in front of the Tontine building. Strangers to Glasgow were always regaled with the story that on the last night of the year, when King Billy heard the hour of twelve strike from the Tron Kirk steeple opposite, he leaped his pawing steed from its pedestal, galloped him down Saltmarket for a drink at the Clyde, and then returned to his position above the heads of the crowd celebrating the New Year.

That was not the only story connected with the statue, and one amusing incident is worth telling. In the early part of the 19th century a Mr Gilmour, well known for his proclivity for practical jokes, was on his way home early one morning from the 'Morning and Evening Club', when he found a ladder in the street. Using it, he climbed on the horse behind the hero of the Boyne. There were very few people about at the early hour, but eventually a man came along who asked Mr Gilmour what he was doing up there. 'Oh I'm looking at the most wonderful sight such as I never saw in all my life before', the joker told him, 'and if you come up you will see it too.' Moved by his natural curiosity, the man climbed on to the top of the pedestal only to be asked to wait a minute until Mr Gilmour could get down from the horse and allow him to mount it. When the dupe was sitting astride the horse Gilmour told him to look steadfastly along the Gallowgate. Then, while the unsuspecting man was thus employed, Gilmour got down from the ladder and removed it, leaving his poor victim stuck up on the horse until somebody could help him down.

Glasgow children had a rhyme about the statue which went like this:

If you want to see King William,
Take a tramway to the Cross,
There you'll see a noble soldier,
Riding on a big black horse.

King Billy astride his horse stood in the Trongate for 189 years — until 1923 when, supposedly because he was obstructing traffic, he was removed to a monumental sculptor's yard until his fate could be decided.

However, there is a much more interesting version of events which goes like this. One Hogmanay, when the crowds around Glasgow Cross were celebrating the New Year and preparing to go on first-footing expeditions, one reveller who had had few drinks too many found himself looking up at a peculiar looking chap astride a horse. As this peculiar looking chap was dressed in just a sheet and looked very unwell indeed, the reveller decided he must bring in the New Year with him and, getting out his bottle from his pocket, started to climb up the plinth and the horse towards King Billy. The cause of what happened next is anybody's guess. Perhaps the weather had eroded the statue, or maybe it was the strength of the reveller. All we do know is that when he grasped the horse's tail a substantial length came off in his hands. This was too much for the reveller, who dropped the tail and ran off. Fortunately, however, some more sober, civic minded citizen retrieved it and returned it to the Corporation. Not long afterwards, the statue, with the tail in a separate parcel, found itself in the yard of Mossman's, the monumental sculptors, where it stayed for three years, until the Town Council decided it should be re-erected in Cathedral Square. That it lacked a good tail posed a bit of a problem, until the ingenious renovators contrived a connecting ball-and-socket arrangement, which meant that every time the wind blew the tail could be seen to move!

So that's how Glasgow came to have a statue with a moving tail; and if you're ever in the region of Cathedral Square, particularly if you have been celebrating, don't worry if you see the tail of King Billy's horse sway; it's not a hallucination; it's not time to contact Alcoholics Anonymous; it really does move.

– 19 –
THE CLYDE'S WORST DISASTER

At 11.20 a.m. on Tuesday 3 July 1883, Alexander Stephen's shipbuilding yard at Linthouse, Govan, was a scene of intense activity as preparations neared completion for the launching of the 500-ton steamer, *Daphne*, ordered by the Glasgow and Londonderry Steam Packet Company to carry passengers and livestock between Northern Ireland and Glasgow. With the yard soon to be closing for the Glasgow Fair Holidays there had been a rush to complete the ship before then, and with only minutes to go before the launch, around 200 men, plumbers, carpenters, engineers, boilermen and their apprentices, were still on board working. Since after the launch the ship was to be towed to the Broomielaw, where her boilers and other furnishings would be fitted; also on board were all the necessary materials for completing the work. Arrangements for the launch were those usually adopted in Clyde shipyards. Slipways were in place, chain cables from the hawse-pipes were fastened to the ground by heavy weights, with just sufficient slack (allowing for the distance the anchors were expected to drag) to pull up the vessel when she reached the middle of the channel. Two steam tugs were standing by to take the steamer to the Broomielaw to be fitted out, and several rowing boats had been put out by the yard as a precaution.

About 11.25 a.m., five minutes before high tide, the naming ceremony began, and as dog-shores were knocked away the *Daphne* began her descent along the slipways towards the waiting waters of the River Clyde. As she entered the water and heeled to port, everyone on board stopped work. They were waiting for her to turn to an even keel and settle. She didn't. After a feeble attempt to right herself she stopped, hung steady for a brief, breathless moment, and then toppled over onto her port side, sinking immediately in the middle of the river.

Fearing what was about to happen, men who had been working on the deck jumped into the water and, although some managed to swim ashore, others were trapped or crushed as the ship came down on top of them. Of those still on board, some were sent sprawling and slipped along the sloping deck into the murky water, where they clung to wooden debris, frantically trying to avoid being sucked into the huge whirlpool caused by the sinking ship. Those who managed to hang onto the port rail were bombarded by the plates and deck planks which had been removed so that the boilers could be lifted into place. Some men were picked up by the steam-tugs and the rowing boats nearby, and unbelievably some were able to await rescue by standing on the *Daphne's* hull which was only a few feet below the surface. Two of the men who helped knock away the dog-shores, Alfred Martin and William Vogwell, had just minutes earlier been aboard the *Daphne*, working beside their two companions, fellow Englishmen, John Lahive and Hendry Clark. All four had come from Devonport just six weeks previously and had been looking forward to sharing the thrill of their first launch. However, a foreman commandeered Martin and Vogwell to help with the dog-shores and, disgruntled, disappointed and envious of everyone on board, they watched the ship move away.

On the other hand, James McLean envied everyone on shore. He didn't know why, but he had a premonition that something dreadful was about to happen, which is why he was working on the deck rather than below and why all morning he had carried a large spar of wood about with him no matter where he went. James's makeshift raft did him no good, for it was wrenched from his hands when the *Daphne* heeled over and he found himself in the water, struggling desperately to keep afloat. God was on his side that day however, and just as his strength was draining away and his worst fear was about to be realised, a line was thrown to him from the tug *Hotspur*. He was then hauled on board — one of the last to be plucked alive from the sudden deadly Clyde.

Although when the vessel heeled over the spectators were paralysed with horror they soon began throwing anything that could float into the water to try to save those who had got clear and were struggling to stay afloat. Five small rowing boats launched from Barclay Curle, the shipyard opposite Stephen's, rescued ten men from drowning, and a workman from the same yard twice dived into the river, saving someone each time.

News of the tragedy spread like wildfire through the streets of Govan and Partick where most of the men employed at Stephen's lived, some in tenements built by the company; and soon there

The Daphne*'s hull lying on her side.*

was a steady stream of wives and mothers pouring into the yard seeking news of husbands, sons, fathers and brothers. The search for bodies began, and at 1.15 p.m. the first was brought ashore. By 2 p.m., divers were on their way and the tide had ebbed, leaving the starboard side of the *Daphne* visible above the surface. By 4 p.m., divers had recovered nine bodies from inside the ship and had reported seeing others trapped within various compartments. Unfortunately, however, as many compartments had small entrances, the divers could not get access for fear of entangling their air tubes. Remember that at the time divers wore large and cumbersome metal helmets.

At the end of the day the temporary mortuary set up in Stephen's joiners' shed held 41 bodies laid out for identification. Among them was a 14-year-old rivet boy, a 25-year old engineer, due to be married the following day, and a 21-year old dentist, William Telfor. William had come to see the launch, and deciding the best place to do so was from the deck of the ship, had asked a workman to smuggle him on board. Once there he had strolled about openly, showing great interest in what was going on. His body was one of the first to be recovered.

As thousands of spectators had joined those awaiting news of relatives and friends the wooden walkways round the yard giving a view of the river were so crowded that it was feared they might collapse, throwing more people into the river. Fortunately, police and staff from Stephen's managed to clear the walkways, averting a further disaster.

On the day after the disaster the Lord Provost of Glasgow received a telegram from Sir Henry Ponsonby on behalf of Queen Victoria which read: 'The Queen hopes that the account of the loss of life is exaggerated. Her Majesty, who is deeply grieved at the disaster, asks if you can give her any further information.' A reply went immediately back to Buckingham Palace, telling her all that had happened and what was being done to retrieve the bodies. The Queen was so moved that she gave a personal cheque for £100 to the disaster fund set up for dependants. By 7 July 75 victims had been recovered and funeral processions were a seemingly unending sight in the streets of Govan and Partick. Stephen's had informed relatives that it would pay the costs of all funeral expenses.

After many attempts the *Daphne* was floated on Thursday 19 July, 17 days after the disaster. The search for bodies then began, and almost immediately four were found in the forecastle (forward part of the upper deck). As they were brought ashore friends and relatives of the missing men waiting by the river side scanned them closely before going to the mortuary to examine the clothing, it being the only means of identification, as the features on the badly decomposed bodies were unrecognisable. As the water got lower and the search was extended, another six bodies were found, making ten in all for the morning's work. Some were found in a crouching position, as though they had been trying to get up from the forehatch where most of them had been working when the vessel heeled over. Many still had tools in their hands. Like those recovered earlier, all the bodies were swollen and decomposed, and before taking them ashore their faces were covered by putting a canvas bag over them. By 1 p.m. the vessel had been removed from mid-channel and an hour later her stern was brought round to within about ten yards of the southern bank. Ambulance men then went on board and disinfected as much of the main deck as they could reach by throwing bucketfuls of disinfectant over it. The members of the Ambulance Corps who had been involved in the search for bodies in the morning courageously went below decks again — with horrifying results. Probing about with boat-hooks immediately below the engine-room skylight, they came upon some soft substances which were evidently bodies. It was a while however, before they could bring out the first of what turned out to be a very long list.

One of the bodies brought ashore was that of 22-year-old John Redpath whose father Archibald had also died. John was identified by his mother and sister, both of whom had travelled to Linthouse every sunrise for 16 weary days to claim first, a husband and father, and then a son and a brother. In this case, as in others, however, the frantic grief witnessed during the first few days in the sad task of claiming the remains of the dead had given place to a quiet resignation. Late on 20 July the *Daphne* was cleared of her dead. Bodies had been discovered in cabins and passageways, behind doors and stairways, and beneath four feet of mud and silt which had gathered in the hold of the sunken ship.

One hundred and twenty-four men lost their lives when the *Daphne* capsized. Of these, six were apprentices aged only 14 and 15. Only 70 of those who had been aboard when the ship heeled over were saved. One of them, rigger Alan McLean, said 'I was standing amidships on the upper deck when the ship heeled over. I got to the high side and when I saw that the vessel was to go down, jumped overboard. I at once struck out for the slip at the yard and after a quarter of an hour's swimming I reached the shore. John Russell was in the water beside me at the time and as he was very exhausted and seemed to be sinking I gave him the preference of the rope.'

Although the official inquiry into the incident, headed by naval architect Sir Edward Reed, cleared the shipbuilders of any blame, the most popular opinion as to the cause of the tragedy was that there were more men working aboard the ship than usual because Stephen's wanted to get her finished ahead of schedule. It was suggested that the time involved with the launch, the towing of the ship to the Broomielaw and the wait for the tradesmen to arrive there from the yard, would have resulted in a precious half-day's work being lost. However, there was nothing unusual in men continuing to work on ships as they were being towed to the harbour for fitting, and at the inquiry it was pointed out that none of the survivors said they were on board by special order of Stephen's.

As to the accusation that Stephen's was trying to finish the ship ahead of schedule, Mr A.R. Brand, representing the owners, told the inquiry that his company was quite satisfied with the progress of the vessel and had not been urging delivery. He said everything was in a very forward state and that they expected her to be delivered very shortly after the launch. On being asked if there was any contract date for delivery he said, 'No, she was ordered on 30th October last year for delivery in about 10 months, strikes excluded.' In answer to the commissioner's question, 'Then she was not overdue?' Brand said, 'She was not. She was not due until the end of August.' When asked if any inducement had been offered to the builders to quicken delivery, Brand admitted that the superintending engineer for his company, William Laing, was authorised, if he saw fit, to advise Stephen's that if overtime was worked assistance would be given in paying the extra wages. In answer to, 'Then, although the builders had no reason under contract for quickening delivery, the owners were desirous of having her as soon as possible?' Brand replied, 'Certainly. We were desirous to have her with as rapid delivery as possible.' After a few more questions it was established that, while there was no formal agreement about Stephen's being compensated for incurring an increase in outlay for quick delivery, the matter had been discussed many times. On giving evidence Mr Alexander Stephen said, 'The arrangement for the launching was made in the usual way as in the case of all our previous 280 ships which were without accident, not so much as a single man ever being hurt.'

There was much discussion about the *Daphne*'s stability and whether her weight had ever been disputed, and on being questioned on this, Robert McMaster, yard manager at Linthouse, said, 'I had many a talk over the matter as I thought the weights were heavy and far above anything we had been in the habit of putting in ships before. Of course, we had never built any ships for the Londonderry people, but with regard to all our castings we had to alter them to suit their design and their method and requirements.' On being asked if he thought there was a good deal of weight aloft in the vessel, he answered, 'Yes, I thought the general outfit altogether was much in excess for the size of the ship. I mentioned some of these matters to Mr John Stephen several times. I used to call his attention to them and say that the weights and wood and everything else were in excess and far more than I anticipated would be inside the ship.'

Sir Edward's report on the inquiry cleared the builders and the owners of the ship of negligence. He said:

> I am thoroughly convinced that neither the builders nor the owners of the ship were in the least degree conscious that any exceptional risk was being incurred by the Daphne's launch, or in the least degree negligent of any precaution which they knew or believed to be essential to its success and safety. Apart from the question of the ship's stability, everything that experience could suggest to secure a safe launch was attended to, and all the arrangements were carried out satisfactorily. I am equally convinced that the system so widely practised by which owners define so many dimensions and particulars of a ship as to leave the designer extremely little scope for determining the elements which regulate a vessel's stability is essentially a bad and dangerous one, causing a division and confusion of responsibility and opening avenues to accidents which neither party foresees.

On the question of whether there was too much loose material on board the vessel, Sir Edward ruled that it was there in the ordinary course of business in order to be fixed as the work progressed, and nothing suggested its possible interference with the vessel's stability or safety.

Sir Edward concluded his report by stating that the complete capsizing of the vessel (notwithstanding the presence of the men and loose materials), was due, in his opinion, solely to lack of stability. He hoped that the lives lost would not have been lost in vain if they aroused shipowners and shipbuilders generally to the fact that the stability of their ship is 'a subject which deserves vastly more consideration than it at present receives'. 'Owners' he said, 'should cease to arrange and settle all those things which determine the ship's stability unless they qualify themselves for the work or employ competent advisers.'

The lives were not lost in vain because, after the disaster, ships had their positions of centre of gravity estimated before launch, their weights aboard assessed, and the number of men limited to those needed for the launch. In fact, the planning of launches reached such a fine art that the final position of large ships on the river could be foretold with great accuracy, as with the Queen Mary, when it was estimated she would travel 1,194 ft but actually covered 1,196 ft.

Repaired and renamed the *Rose,* the *Daphne* plied the Irish Channel between Ireland and Scotland for many years before going aground in the Firth of Clyde. Refloated, her wearied owners sold her to the Mediterranean trade, where she became the *Ianthe*. Again she went aground. In 1923, under a fourth name *Elani*, the unluckiest ship of the Clyde was scrapped.

Despite the tragedy being one of the most appalling in the history of world shipbuilding, it remained largely forgotten until 1996 when descendants of those who died won a battle to create a lasting tribute to the men from Govan and Partick who perished. On Sunday 8 December members of the Govan Reminiscence Group and representatives of Glasgow City Council joined the relatives to unveil two identical bronze memorial plaques featuring the hull of the *Daphne*. Designed by a local man, John McArthur, the plaques were unveiled in two separate ceremonies on either side of the Clyde — Elder Park to the south and the Victoria Park rose gardens to the north. As a touching token to the memory of the men who died, the niece of one of them, Netta Carruthers from Govan, scattered 124 roses from Glasgow's Bell's Bridge into the water below. Netta said that she remembered stories of the tragedy, and that it had almost claimed her grandfather as well as her 19-year-old uncle. 'He had a very lucky escape', she said. 'He was a foreman and got off just an hour before the *Daphne* was launched.' Apart from a headstone in Cardonald Cemetery, commemorating eight of the dead, the plaques are the only permanent memorials. Mrs Carruthers blamed the long wait for a memorial on the reluctance of the shipbuilders to face up to mistakes that may have been at the root of the tragedy (Alexander Stephen's yard closed in 1968).

Although the Govan Reminiscence Group had been researching for more than two years they still did not know all the facts. Their Chairman, Thomas Stewart, said: 'We could find so little information about what happened; it was surprising. We have had reports that one of the owners of the shipbuilders was with the police, and that this was maybe why it was quietened down.' Only one month after the tragedy, all mention of the capsize and the deaths ceased in the press and to this day no-one knows what happened to the fund set up for the families. I suppose no-one will ever find out the true story, but there certainly did seem to be a 'cover-up': despite the fact that much of the evidence given at the inquiry seemed to incriminate the shipbuilders and the owners, they were both exonerated from any blame.

– 20 –
GLASGOW SAYS FAREWELL
TO THE LEERIES

On 1 September 1971 Glasgow's only remaining gas street lamp, in North Portland Place, Townhead, was ceremoniously lit by Lord Provost Sir Donald Liddle in the presence of 12 of the longest serving 'leeries' (lamplighters) in the city with 356 years' service between them. Sir Donald was later presented with a shortened version of a 'leerie' pole (used to ignite the gas) by Hugh Creane, who had been with the lighting department for 38 years. While no-one seriously wanted to return to the days of gas lighting, for the people attending the ceremony it was a nostalgic occasion tinged with sadness, as it meant that the once familiar figure of the lamplighter with his ladder on his shoulder and his lighting pole would no longer be seen lighting street lamps. In fact, one guest, the manager of the Scottish Gas Board, said he felt he was attending a wake. Although there were still lamplighters in the city who did their rounds each night, they were no longer called lamplighters, or leeries. They were officially known as 'public lighting maintenance engineers' with the dual role of attending to gas and electric stair lamps.

The recollection most people have of leeries is that they always seemed to be so small in stature that their ability to carry both a ladder and a pole was a source of wonder. Small or not, the public had a warm affection for them, possibly because they brought light into dark streets, making the city a brighter, safer place. Such was the popularity of leeries that poets were moved to write about them:

> Carrying a magic wand,
> Like a sceptre beaming,
> Up the street the leerie comes,
> A' the lamps are gleaming.

The leeries were prime targets for unruly boys, who taunted them, knowing that they couldn't chase them, being hampered with their ladder and pole. A favourite game in Glasgow streets was to wait for the leerie to light the lamps in one street, then climb up the lamp-posts, blow the lights out and then, from a safe distance, tell the leerie what had been done. Another trick was to take the mercury out of the lamps, which meant that they wouldn't light.

While the last street gas light was being removed, lighting specialists were talking of floodlighting to remove the drabness of the concrete in modern redevelopments and they were experimenting in Anderston, hoping it would give life to buildings that appeared dead in darkness. Councillor Thomas Fulton, convener of the Highways Committee, forecast that 'some day the evening skyline in Glasgow will be something wonderful to see.' He was right. It is.

The history of Glasgow's street lamps is fascinating, indeed 'illuminating' if you will pardon the pun. Erected in 1718, the first lamps had tallow wicks but, as there were so few and the light given was feeble, people who could afford it either carried their own lamps or had a servant to light the way when walking out in the dark. By 1765 streets were lit by oil lamps but, possibly through influence, many of them found their way to private closes. Accordingly, the magistrates ordered the lamps the council supplied with oil to be removed to the streets for general use. In 1780, as a reward for proprietors laying pavements opposite their premises, the council placed nine lamps on the south side of the Trongate, from the Tron Church steeple to Stockwell Street, and offered to extend the line of lamps west if the proprietors there also laid pavements. Lots of pavements must have been laid, because by 1815 the city had 1,274 lamps. The Glasgow Gaslight Company, authorised in 1817 to manufacture gas for supply to the city and for lighting the streets, introduced gas lighting to Glasgow the following year, when 1,472 streets lamps were lit with the new luminant. From then on growth progressed by various stages from the use of one burner to multiple burners.

Incidentally, on 5 September 1818, grocer James Hamilton, 128 Trongate, gave the first public exhibition of the new product with six 'jetties' which he had fitted up in his shop. Immediately afterwards gas was introduced into the Theatre Royal in Dunlop Street, and on 18 September, when the large crystal lustre in the roof was turned on, the audience thought for a moment they had been ushered into another world.

The 1866 Glasgow Police Act authorised the council to 'erect and maintain lamps and lamp-posts and other appurtenances for lighting in a suitable manner all public and private streets, courts and common stairs within the city; to light the dial-plates of turret clocks and city timepieces and to appoint an inspector of lighting to take charge of that work and be responsible for the good conduct of the lamplighters and others appointed by him.' In February 1893, the council installed the first electric street light and by 1971, when the last gas lamp disappeared, there were 52,879.

Sad though losing the leerie was, the ending of gas lighting in Glasgow's streets brought the lighting department a boom they hadn't quite expected — the sale of lamp-posts. 'We have supplied lampposts to almost every place in the world' said Mr Colvin, the city lighting engineer, 'particularly to America and Canada. The lamplighters' poles are also in great demand as souvenirs.'

Nowadays, with buildings floodlit and streets and stairs lit by electricity controlled by computers, gas lamps and leeries, like the tramcar driver, have been consigned to the history books.

– 21 –
POLICE INSPECTOR SHOT DEAD
IN HIGH STREET

The above headline goes back to 1921 when the fight for Irish independence was at its height. For almost two years from the day the Republic of Ireland set up its own Parliament in 1919, a state of guerilla warfare had existed between the Irish and the British Army, the Irish fighting with ambush, assassination and murder, for which they were hanged when caught by the British. There was great bitterness on both sides, and hardly a day passed without newspaper reports of raids, murders, kidnappings and jailbreaks. With the fight reaching its climax and the Irish Free State just about to come into being, the Sinn Feiners and the Irish Republican Army were involved in hundreds of clashes with the army and the police, not all of them on Irish soil, which brings us to the murder of the police inspector in Glasgow's High Street.

The day of the murder, 4 May 1921, began like any other with men, women and children going about their business as usual. Although later, with hindsight, some people would remember seeing suspicious-looking men loitering around the walls of Duke Street Prison, at the time they paid no attention to them. If they had, they might have seen that they were anxiously watching the junction of Drygate with High Street, their hats pulled low and their hands stuffed into jacket pockets. What the men were waiting for was a police van ferrying prisoners from the Central Police Court in St Andrew's Square to Duke Street Prison. However, although there were two prisoners in the van, the men were only interested in one, Frank J. Carty, alias Frank Somers, a commandant in the Sligo branch of the Irish Republican Army. Carty had been arrested for the theft of firearms in Ireland and twice had been rescued from jail. After his second escape he had made his way to Glasgow and was arrested there on 28 April 1921.

During the hostilities, cities throughout the United Kingdom were alerted to be on the lookout for Irish revolutionaries, and as Glasgow had many Irish sympathisers the police were frequently called upon to search people suspected of possessing firearms, ammunition or revolutionary literature. They were also asked to arrest Irish fugitives, which is how Carty came to be arrested and charged with the theft of a revolver in Sligo and jail-breaking. Following his arrest Carty was twice remanded in custody at the Central Police Court, the second time being on 4 May when he was committed to Duke Street Prison for four days. His removal to the prison posed a problem however, as it was feared his comrades would attempt to rescue him as they had done before. Because of that, the police took no chances. Carty and the other prisoner, a nonentity charged with indecent assault, were locked in separate compartments of the police van, escorted by Constables George Bernard and David Brown. The driver of the van was Constable Thomas Ross, and in front beside him were Inspector Robert Johnston and Detective Sergeant George Stirton with Detective Constable Murdoch Macdonald seated behind. Stirton and Macdonald carried revolvers.

The van, which left the Central Police Station about midday, was minutes later climbing High Street towards Cathedral Square. Everything was fine until it had almost reached the prison and then, entirely without warning, about thirty armed men ran out of Rottenrow, dividing into three groups as they advanced. With great presence of mind Ross kept the van moving and as he turned into Cathedral Square the first shots were fired. They came from the rear, but seconds later one of the groups lined up on the south pavement and opened fire on the nearside of the vehicle. Ross drew up and Stirton began firing through the windscreen, telling Johnston to take cover as he was in the line of fire. His warning was too late — two more shots were fired; Johnston sagged forward and tipped over sideways on to the street. He was shot through the heart and died almost immediately.

Stirton, revolver in hand, jumped down and, standing over his colleague's body, blasted away at his attackers until a bullet shattered his right wrist. Meanwhile Macdonald was engaged in a fierce battle with the gunmen and then, hearing shots from the rear of the van, ran round to see what was happening. He found gunmen firing at the door locks and, despite his revolver being empty, he made straight for them. Foiled in their attempt to open the van and get Carty out, the gunmen began to withdraw, knowing that the sound of the gun battle would have alerted the prison. They separated, some making their way along Rottenrow,

The rear of the police van showing a bullet-hole in the lock and the splintered panelling.

others down the Drygate and into Cathedral Square, all calmly melting into the crowds. The wounded Stirton ran after some of them but had lost too much blood to pursue them very far. When he returned to where Johnston lay an ex-nurse rushed to help him but he said, 'Don't mind me any more missus. Go and help my chum.' The woman knelt beside Johnston sprawled on the ground in a pool of blood and immediately knew that he was beyond help.

Despite Macdonald seeing a man shot dead and having been involved in a gun battle at a range of yards, he had the wits afterwards to arrest the driver of a delivery van standing nearby on the off-chance that the van was there to help Carty escape. How driver Ross, unarmed and still at the wheel, escaped death, was a mystery, as during the gunfight bullets rattled against the van with three piercing the radiator and several going through the windscreen. However, against all the odds he did, and while the gunmen were vanishing from the scene he managed to start the van and, with Stirton and Macdonald walking beside it, steered it through the prison gates. On trying to open the van's damaged rear door it was found that the lock had jammed and it took the combined efforts of several big policemen to force it and let the passengers out — passengers who were lucky to be alive, as the bullets fired into the lock had bounced around the interior of the van. Stirton was taken to the Royal Infirmary and Macdonald was miraculously unhurt.

The description of events conjures up a picture of a lengthy gunfight. But it wasn't. It all happened in the space of seconds — the crash of the revolvers, the terror of the people, the collapse of the inspector and the escape of the gunmen. News of the rescue attempt and Johnston's murder, which became known as 'The Glasgow Atrocity', created a sensation in the West of Scotland. People were alarmed as it meant that the violent goings-on over the water had suddenly landed on their doorstep.

The police started their search for the gunmen, relentlessly seeking out and interrogating every person suspected of being connected with the Sinn Fein Movement and, as their investigations grew, it became evident that the organisation's underground was much more extensive than was ever imagined. Their enquiries centred on the city's East End, and after receiving tip-offs, they swooped on some flats in Abercrombie Street, Bridgeton. The information was accurate. When Detective-Lieutenant John Forbes forced open a cellar at No. 74 he unearthed the largest haul of arms and explosives ever found in Glasgow. There were 35 revolvers, six hand-grenades, a bomb, many pounds of gelignite, a large number of detonators, eight bags of percussion caps, 955 rounds of revolver and rifle ammunition, holsters, magazines, a bayonet and a coil of fuse wire.

When it became known that arrests had been made a crowd gathered outside. At the time, the police were neither liked nor trusted in the area, and when they dragged their prisoners outside the mob threw stones and demonstrated — what was described at the time as — 'their keen indignation'. Over the next few hours the keen indignation grew until there was a 2,000-strong mob of furious men and women thronging the streets. Before the police managed to disperse the crowd, shop windows were broken, police officers were assaulted, a tram was vandalised and soldiers were sent to protect the Central Police Office, fearing it would be attacked. At the end of the inquiries 34 people were arrested, charged with (1) attempting to rescue a prisoner and discharging loaded firearms (2) killing Inspector Johnston and (3) wounding Detective Sergeant Stirton. While all that was going on Frank J. Carty was deported to Ireland.

Of the 34 originally charged, only 13 men were sent to the High Court in Edinburgh for trial, one of them having so many names that he had to be charged under three different ones. Against each of the accused the Crown listed an additional charge of conspiracy, making four charges in all. All pleaded 'not guilty' when the trial opened on 8 August 1921.

Detective Sergeant Stirton's account of the attack was the most graphic. He said that he and Detective Constable Macdonald had only been issued with revolvers on the strictest instructions not to use them unless attacked. He then told the court that when the van was about 15 yards from Drygate he heard a shot coming from its rear and simultaneously three men came from the direction of the prison wall. The men lined up on the pavement and, resting their revolvers on their left arms, opened fire on the van. He positively identified nine of the accused. Macdonald corroborated his evidence and identified six of the accused. However, in the atmosphere of plot and counterplot and assumed names, it was obvious that a verdict of guilty would be impossible. All the accused pleaded alibis which the jury accepted. Six were found not guilty and the charges against the others were found not proven.

Although the giant, dark, forbidding Duke Street Prison is now gone, parts of the wall can still be seen on the housing scheme which replaced it, and if you look carefully, using a bit of imagination, you can still find the marks left by the bullets on the day of 'The Glasgow Atrocity'.

– 22 –
RIOT IN THE COLISEUM THEATRE

When Dr Walford Bodie MD, an illusionist and hypnotist with pretensions to be a healer, was booked to appear at the Glasgow Coliseum for the week beginning 11 November 1909, he had no idea he would be the cause of the greatest student riot ever known in Scotland. The circumstances leading to the riot started a week before, when Charles Henry Irving brought an action to recover £1,000 from Samuel Murphy Bodie, professionally known as 'Dr Walford Bodie', hypnotist, mesmerist, bloodless surgeon and medical electrician. Irving said that Bodie had promised to teach him all he knew but that he had discovered that it was all trickery and fraud.

Bodie lost the case and had to pay back Irving's £1,000. However, as it had been proved that his 'cures' were fakes, and that his hypnotic subjects travelled round with him from theatre to theatre, he lost more than money; his reputation vanished like a puff of smoke. On being asked why he put the letters MD after his name he replied that they stood for 'Merry Devil'. He did claim to have doctorates from two American Colleges — colleges which nobody could trace. With his coal black hair, waxed moustache, curving upwards like little horns and his cloak billowing behind him, Bodie epitomised most people's conception of the devil.

Because the Great Bodie was due to appear the following week at the Coliseum Music Hall, the case created an even greater sensation in Glasgow than anywhere else. The theatre advertised 'The Famous Bloodless Surgeon', adding, to cover itself 'The Management disclaim any responsibility for any statement made by Dr Bodie.' Round the Coliseum entrance were hung crutches, limb-supports and all manner of medical aids to serious illness. These, it was announced, were the implements which had belonged to the vast number of people 'cured' by Dr Bodie. On Monday night the theatre was packed at the first house, and when the curtain rose on the Great Bodie the atmosphere was electric on both sides of the footlights. Despite the manager having made an appeal for law and order the minute Bodie appeared he was greeted with booing, hissing and a chant which became very familiar over the next few days — 'Bodie! Bodie! Quack, quack, quack! Bodie! Bodie! Quack, quack quack!'. When Bodie started speaking he became the target for a barrage of missiles, including eggs and bags of peasemeal which gave off a white fog when they burst. Although some missiles found their mark Bodie managed to go through his act but was hooted off the stage. At the second house there was another row, but nothing was thrown and Bodie told the audience that he was ashamed to be Scotch.

There was more trouble at the theatre on Tuesday night. Medical students occupied the circle, and at the second house they greeted everything Bodie did with hisses. 'This is my seventeenth visit to the city' Bodie said, 'and I have always been greeted well, ladies and gentlemen.' He then pointed to the circle and shouted with scorn, 'I can't call these gentlemen, but what can be expected from people who cadge Carnegie grants?' The insult was greeted with such a storm of booing and hissing that Bodie had to leave the stage. At a meeting at Gilmorehill the students decided to demand an apology from the Great Bodie and the next evening they marched to the Coliseum dressed in old clothes and carrying heavy walking sticks.

At the first house (and as it turned out the only house) there were 1,500 students in the audience of 3,000. Fifty policemen were also there by invitation from the theatre manager. The audience greeeted every act that evening with wild applause, but when Bodie's was announced a deafening yell of condemnation broke out, and when he appeared leading his assistant La Belle Electra by the hand, all hell broke loose. Rotten eggs, apples, days' old kippers, bags of peasemeal and other objects were tossed at the stage, which was soon inches thick with rubbish. Although Bodie and La Belle Electra fled and the fire curtain was lowered, still the bombardment went on against the curtain and on the heads of the cowering orchestra. Fighting broke out between the students and the police all over the theatre, and then about twenty students rushed the stage, one tearing a hole in the curtain. What happened next was like something from a Keystone Kops silent movie. From the other side of the curtain came a brush-stick, knocking the student headlong into the orchestra pit, and then policemen poured through the hole in the curtain. Fortunately, before any more damage was done or someone was injured, a man with a powerful voice stood up on a stall seat and managed to obtain comparative silence. He turned out to be an ex-president of the student's Union and he appealed to the students not to wreck the theatre, saying he would ask Bodie to apologise. Bodie agreed, although no-one could hear him through the chants of 'Bodie! Bodie! Quack, quack, quack!'.

Four students were arrested. The others formed up outside the theatre and marched through the town to the West End, intending to call on a Professor Eastburn and a Dr Macara. However, the police got there first and lined up in front of each gentleman's house. There was more fighting and another student was arrested. That was the end of Bodie's appearances at the Coliseum, as the management cancelled his contract. It was in fact the end of his career in No. 1 theatres where he had been earning £300 a week. While the students hadn't killed him, they certainly killed his extravagant lifestyle.

Hailed as heroes, the Glasgow students received telegrams of congratulation from Aberdeen and Leeds Universities and one from the London medical students, saying 'Please leave a bit of Bodie for us.' Billed to appear the following week in London, the Great Bodie expediently had a 'nervous breakdown'.

The student riot was not the end of the Bodie affair in Glasgow. He was further baited by 200 apprentice engineers marching through Glasgow on the Monday after his first appearance, carrying banners and a 'coffin'. They got no further than the Jamaica Bridge, when the police broke up their procession.

When the arrested students appeared in court public opinion was firmly behind them, and they gained even more support when Brodie (as a witness) again asserted that the letters MD, after his name, stood for 'Merry Devil'. The students were found guilty, fined a derisory amount, became heroes, and the incident was enshrined in local folklore as the 'Bodie Riot'. Incidentally, one of the students was Osborne H. Mavor, who later gave up medicine, changed his name to James Bridie, became a playwright, and went on to found the Citizens Theatre.

– 23 –
A.E. PICKARD UNLIMITED

Mr Albert Ernest Pickard was the last of Glasgow's great eccentrics, a man who bucked the establishment and had a compulsive wish to shock or amuse the public with his outrageous behaviour. Eccentric he may have been; a fool he was not. His business accumen and showmanship made him a millionaire, and there are so many stories to tell about the little man in the old-fashioned knickerbocker suit, battered soft hat and pebble glasses who was for sixty years a familiar figure in Glasgow, that it's difficult to know where to start.

Pickard, who styled himself 'A.E. Pickard Unlimited of London, Paris, Moscow and Bannockburn', was born in Bradford in 1874. He started his working life in the printing business, but not liking it very much he began an engineering apprenticeship. He didn't like that much either, and after trying this and that he eventually found regular employment repairing carnival penny-in-the slot machines. Gradually he began putting his own show stands together and took them, particularly rifle ranges, to London, Paris, Lyons, Marseilles and Monte Carlo. He even came to Glasgow once. It is possible that fond memories of Glasgow were in Pickard's mind in 1904 when he came across an advertisement that Fell's Waxworks in the Trongate were for sale; but whatever it was he sold his rifle ranges and arrived in the city on 1 May.

Pickard didn't think much of Fell's Waxworks but, feeling there were possibilities he handed over his cheque for £437 10s to Mr Fell. Fell's Waxworks became Pickard's American Museum, and as well as having wax dummies on show Pickard introduced live acts. He also began advertising his attractions which other waxworks' owners didn't bother doing. Shortly after buying Fell's Waxworks Pickard bought the small Gaiety Theatre in Elgin Street, Clydebank. 'That's when I started collecting property', he once told a reporter in his rasping, aggressive Yorkshire accent that he never lost.

What really put Pickard's American Museum on the map, making it the sensation of Glasgow, was Monsieur Victor Beaute, the fasting man. Beaute, a professional faster, weighed 11st 7lb on

A.E. Pickard dressed in his favourite outfit.

1 October 1906 when he went into a cage at 101 Trongate to make his attempt on the world's fasting record, standing at 40 days. Allowed only cigarettes and aerated water, his wooden cage with windows on each side was divided into two by curtains. One part had a bedstead, the other, an armchair, a small chair, a table and a chest of drawers. There was no door, and when Beaute stepped through a *window* it was immediately sealed.

From day one crowds flocked to see the fasting man, and every day Pickard put up a new giant notice — *Mons Beaute's 18th Day of his World Record Fast,* changing it to 19th, 20th and so on. A doctor attended Beaute every day, and on the 39th day, when his weight had dropped to 8st 11lb, Glasgow's magistrates decided something had to be done, and they told Pickard that he would be held criminally responsible if Beaute died. Pickard and his lawyer assured the magistrates that the fast would end at midnight that evening, which it did, with Beaute still looking hale and hearty. Sceptics said that the ebony cane Beaute carried was hollow and was filled with a large supply of concentrated beef tablets. Despite not breaking the world record the event was a triumph for Pickard — a masterstroke of showmanship.

Early on Pickard believed that his future lay in the entertainment business (understandable, considering his outrageously zany sense of humour and flair for publicity) and in 1906 he bought the old Britannia Music Hall above his Waxworks, renaming the whole complex The Panopticon. 'It means', he said 'a place where you can see everything'. An example of Pickard's peculiar sense of humour was the large sign outside the Panopticon reading, 'Mind the Step'. There was no step of course. It was just his idea of fun, his maxim, which he was always quoting, being, 'You've got to 'ave a bit o' fun, you know, life's all fun.'

Dressed in Japanese outfits, the ladies' orchestra that played for the acts in the music hall had the only seats in the house. The audience had to stand. Performers were often amateurs, and Pickard always declared proudly that he was partly responsible for the fame of Laurel and Hardy, as the teenager, Stan Jefferson, later Stan Laurel, made a very early stage appearance in the Panopticon. Young Stan had ambitions to be a comedian, and when Pickard agreed to give him a chance he went on stage with jokes and comedy routines he had heard at the Metropole Theatre in Stockwell Street which his father managed. The Music Hall had four shows daily and, not being exactly upmarket, was a rowdy house, with the audience often throwing rotten fruit and vegetables at performers who failed to please. Pickard had his own inimitable way of dealing with rowdy patrons. He sat at the top of a ladder at the side of the stage throwing screw nails at those exceeding the permitted bounds of rowdiness.

On first nights and during Friday night's 'Amateur Hour' he usually positioned himself at the side of the stage armed with a long pole with a hook at the end large enough to encircle a man's neck. With this, much to the delight of the audience, he yanked from the stage any aspiring artiste that failed to come up to the modest standards of the Panopticon. Often he did the poor performers a favour by hooking them off, thereby saving them from a barrage of rotting fruit and vegetables and verbal abuse from the unappreciative theatregoers. Amateur Night at the Panopticon was such a riot that the 2d seats cost 4d that evening.

Pickard's Museum and Waxworks ran four shows daily, featuring realistic scenes and figures in wax, a torture chamber, sideshows, a shooting gallery, laughing mirrors, tattooing saloons and freaks of all kinds, on which he was an expert, scrutinising the papers daily for news of them. There was Alice Bounds, the Bear Woman of Texas. Alice was coloured, walked on all fours, and was covered with thick hair like a bear. Nevertheless, on looking back Pickard said he was inclined to think that she was wearing a bearskin. There was also Tom Thumb, the successor to the original General Tom Thumb, but 12 inches smaller. He was Harold Pyott of Stockport and was 23 inches tall and weighed 24lbs. As well as a Bearded Lady, there was a Half-Lady and an Armless Wonder.

However, Pickard's greatest achievement was the bringing of the Mullingar Leprechaun to his museum. In 1908 reports came from Ireland that children at Mullingar had seen a leprechaun (a fairy who guards a pot of gold) and immediately a search began for it. Eventually it was caught and held in the Mullingar workhouse. Pickard lost no time, and before anyone could draw breath he had the leprechaun at his Waxworks, publicised by a giant poster proclaiming:

The Cry of the City

Have you seen the Leprechaun?
The Mullingar Fairy
The only one ever captured alive
Irish Patriot...A.E. Pickard

Crowds rushed to see the leprechaun, a dwarf-like figure sitting in a cage rocking himself to and fro or picking the works out of clocks. His speech was peculiar, a cross between a grunt and a squeak, and although he had been naked when found and had torn off two sets of clothes during his trip from Ireland to Glasgow, he had taken to wearing six jackets in which he stowed his pieces of clock.

Pickard always maintained that he introduced the 'talkies' to Britain by buying an instrument called the Chronograph. 'Bioscope and phonograph are combined' said a reporter at the time, 'the

The Panoptican building in Argyle Street.

artist being shown on the screen while the machine plays the song which he is singing.' That was in December 1906, and Pickard continued to show talking pictures until the supply ran dry.

Although the Panopticon was doing well, in 1908 Pickard decided to compete with a most influential showman in Glasgow, E.H. Bostock, who ran the Scottish Zoo in New City Road. He turned a cellar below the theatre into a zoo, called it Pickard's Noah's Ark and to publicise his new venture he drove a lorry decorated to represent Noah's Ark round the city. As it only cost 2d to get into Noah's Ark against 6d to get into the Scottish Zoo, and the Trongate was in the centre of the town, and New City Road was slightly out of town, Bostock naturally worried about the competition. A battle between Bostock and Pickard then began.

Bostock objected to Pickard's title, saying that the Wombell Menagerie had been using it before Pickard was even heard of. He then started advertising 'The Scottish Zoo! — the Only Zoological Collection in Scotland Worthy of the Name. A Veritable Noah's Ark!' 'Ark! I hear the Lions Roar', started Pickard in his next advertisement. 'Noah's Ark and Glasgow Zoo adjoining the Panopticon. The finest Zoological Collection Ever Exhibited. 20 Cages of Wild Animals, Monkeys' Home and Birds' Paradise, Explorer...A.E. Pickard Unlimited.' In one advertisement Pickard printed the slogan 'Truth is a rock upon which all may stand'. Bostock retaliated by stating 'Monkeys and parrots do not constitute a zoo.'

Pickard had an eagle which escaped, and Bostock had an elephant which went mad and had to be shot. Pickard had a bear which got loose and had to be shot too! But, whereas Bostock had to turn out the army to shoot his elephant, Pickard shot his bear himself.

The battle might have gone on forever, but the fact was that the New City Zoo was not doing well, and a year later all the animals were sold. Bostock changed the place into a gigantic roller skating rink, leaving Pickard free to advertise his Noah's Ark as the only zoo in Glasgow. Pickard didn't believe in being magnanimous and had at the foot of his advertisement, 'Man and Beast Tamer...A. E. Pickard'. Pickard did try to open a roller skating rink also, but he had to give up the idea as he couldn't get a suitable building, and Bostock had taken the precaution of buying up all the pairs of roller skates on the market.

At the beginning of the First World War Pickard decided that the future of the entertainment business in Glasgow lay in the cinema, and by the time it was well under way he had sold the Gaiety Theatre in Clydebank and had built his first cinema, the Casino, at Townhead. It was a gold mine, and because of its success he built the Seamore Palace in Maryhill Road. Although his cinemas were taking up most of his time he didn't neglect the Panopticon, and back in April 1915 he was advertising, 'The declared ambition of the Kaiser, before being despatched to St Helena, is to visit the Panopticon.' For his waxworks he advertised 'a Half Lady and 999,999 other Freaks, including the Kaiser'. However, an advertisement of 1916 iillustrated the popularity of 'the pictures':

BUSINESS AS USUAL
PICKARD'S SEAMORE PALACE
UNUSUAL BUSINESS
PICKARD'S TOWNHEAD CASINO
EXTRA BUSINESS
PICKARD'S PANOPTICON
ROTTEN BUSINESS

With variety acts being put on as an added attraction to films instead of films being an added attraction to variety shows, Pickard turned the Panopticon into a cinema and built a new place, The Black Cat, in Springfield Road.

It was around this time that Pickard began the business that made him a millionaire, buying and selling property all over Glasgow. After Glasgow Corporation he was the biggest landlord in the city. 'Does Glasgow belong to me?' he once shouted at an interviewer, 'Of course it does!'. When Will Fyffe began singing it belonged to him, Pickard threatened to take out an action against him in the Court of Session.

In 1961, after fifty active years in the property business, Pickard announced that he didn't know how many properties he owned or how much money he was worth. He did admit he was a millionaire. Such was his expertise in buying property that, if a particular building interested him, no-one thought it worthwhile bidding against him, as the following story illustrates:

One day Pickard was in Greenock on his way to Rothesay when he met a fellow property dealer. The man paled when he saw Albert Ernest: 'I didn't know you knew about this', he blurted out. Pickard didn't have a clue what the man was talking about but managed to look knowing. 'Here' said the chap desperately. 'I'll give you £100 if you stay out of the bidding. What about it?' Pickard was thinking the conversation over when the man counted out £100 saying 'For any favour Mr Pickard, give us a chance. Just take this and leave it to us.' Pickard took the notes and went on his way wondering what it was all about. He hadn't known anything about a building for sale in Greenock.

Pickard's property deals were not all trouble free. He was involved in various legal actions concerning his unorthodox wheeling and dealing. When Pickard built his biggest cinema at Shawlands in 1927, he ran a competition to pick the name and characteristically chose 'The White Elephant'. It was hugely popular, and on noticeboards throughout the city were arrowed directions 'To Pickard's White Elephant Cinema via Bridgeton Cross and Jerusalem'. Apart from its size, what made the White Elephant different from any other cinema was what Pickard called 'neuks'. Each neuk seated two people who could see the screen if they wanted to but were completed hidden from the rest of the audience. 'I didn't like to see young couples doing their courting in closes' he said, 'I thought it would be better to have them doing it in my cinema.' When Pickard sold the cinema in 1934 for £40,000, the new owner removed the neuks. He also sold the Seamore for £30,000, and when a reporter asked him why he had sold his cinemas Pickard told him that the worry of owning them was putting him off his golf.

Obviously he had not got the cinema bug out of his system, for a year later he bought the Norwood Dance Hall near Charing Cross and turned it into a cinema. Pickard opened it in a peculiar manner, although to him it probably seemed perfectly normal. Having positioned himself across the road with a large piece of wood tucked under his arm he charged across the road and, using the wood as a battering ram, burst open the cinema's doors. He then declared it open to the public. This time arrowed directions were unnecessary to find his new cinema, for he had placed a huge model of the Forth Bridge on its roof. Later Pickard renamed it the Crystal Palace, because of all the glass he had put in it. When he sold it in 1945 his long association with the cinema business ended.

An amusing anecdote of Pickard's cinema days was when David Gouk, who worked for Pathé in Glasgow, made an appointment to meet him at the White Elephant to persuade him to buy a new film. When Gouk arrived there was a great crowd outside the building gaping at Pickard who, dressed in opera cloak and hat, was sitting on top of a desk that was on top of a table. Business was then conducted with Gowk standing on the pavement.

I should probably not have called that anecdote amusing: 'interesting' might have been more appropriate, since not everyone found Pickard's behaviour amusing, for example, a firm of London builders employed by him to do a job costing £5,000 — no small sum in those days. When Pickard received an invoice for the work he immediately sent back a telegram reading 'Please attend

The Elephant Cinema at Shawlands.

creditors' meeting in Glasgow tomorrow. Pickard.' Simultaneously he signed a cheque for £5,000 and sent it off to London. Within an hour there was a frantic phone call from the builders. The head of the firm had received Pickard's telegram and had gone home to lie down. Pickard tried to explain that the telegram was just his idea of fun and that a cheque was in the post. He was often genuinely disappointed when the rest of the world didn't share his sense of fun.

Albert Edward was the first man in Glasgow to buy a private aeroplane and the first to buy a large motor car fitted with glass which no-one outside could see through. He was also the first man in the city to be fined for parking. It happened when he was late for a cinema trade outing to Rothesay and only managed to catch his train by parking his car in the middle of Platform 8 in Central Station. He was fined £1, which he paid with a £100 note. The incident of course got him maximum publicity.

While Pickard relished being the centre of attention, he wasn't so keen on other people being in the limelight, especially some Scots celebrities. He had a down on Sir Harry Lauder and Will Fyffe, arguing that they had no right to represent Scots as comic figures. To get back at them he went as far as to appear in the street dressed in a terrible tartan suit specially made for him.

Despite Pickard's high profile he was unsuccessful in being elected to Glasgow Town Council. He had tried several times, but being essentially a loner and an aggressive self-publicist didn't endear him to people. Also, his great showman rival, E. H. Bostock, was a councillor and a Justice of the Peace. In 1951 he made another attempt to be elected to public office by standing for Parliament as 'The Independent Millionaire Candidate' for the Maryhill Division. Although he thought he would be elected because 'I own most of Maryhill' he was unsuccessful, polling only 356 votes and losing his £150 deposit. William Hannan, who won the seat, got 22,912 votes and Paul Cowcher, the runner-up, 13,076. The defeated candidate's only remark was 'We've added a little bit of fun to the election.'

At one time Pickard had eight cars — 'one for each day, and two for Sundays', he said. They ranged from a Rolls Royce to his favourite Chevrolet with the licence plate G2. A huge bell labelled 'A.E.P's Church Bell, 19½ cwts' decorated the Chevrolet. 'Lovely isn't it' Pickard would say happily. 'Everybody thinks it's the real bell from the church I bought in Bath Street and demolished. Daft, eh? How could a car support 19½ hundredweights? This bell's made out of wood by one of my chaps.'

One thing Pickard kept quiet was his family life. He lived with his second wife, a daughter and two sons in a Victorian town house in Belhaven Terrace in Glasgow's West End. Belhaven Terrace however, was not his only home in the West End. He owned the palatial Golden Gates mansion in Great Western Road, named because of the two enormous ornamental gates at the entrance, which he had made in a blacksmith's shop in Lochburn Road, Maryhill.

Even in death Albert Ernest Pickard made headlines. At the age of 90 he died in a fire at his house in Belhaven Terrace. He was an extraordinary character, aggressive, boastful, deadly serious in business, but with a hatred of snobs and pompous people. He also had a heart; none of his tenants were ever evicted from any of his properties, and he secretly gave generously to charities. It's possible, like so many extroverts, that his outrageous behaviour was a front and that underneath he had feelings of inadequacy stemming from his deprived early life, lack of formal education and lack of inches. If that were true, and he had a king-size 'I'll-show-them' complex: he certainly put on a first-class act and he certainly did show them. 'Mr Popularity' he may not have been, but Pickard was missed by many Glaswegians who were in the habit of asking 'What's he up to now?'. Glasgow was a duller place without him, because, 'You've got to 'ave a bit o' fun, you know, life's all fun.'

– 24 –
BLACK DAYS IN SOCCER HISTORY

There have been many black days in soccer history, but three of the blackest happened in Glasgow — two at Ibrox Park and one at Hampden. As the first was in 1902, the second in 1909 and the third in 1971, I'm going to tell the stories in that order.

1902: Disaster in the Ibrox Stand

On 5 April 1902, frenzied cheering spectators caused what was, at the time, the worst disaster in the history of football. It happened in the opening minutes of the 31st International match between Scotland and England at Ibrox Park, when a section of a wooden platform collapsed on the sloping western terrace, and hundreds of people hurtled to the ground — a sheer drop of forty feet. To escape from the yawning gap spectators spilled on to the pitch, but curiously, although there were 60,000 people at Ibrox, only those on the fringe of the tragedy were aware of it. The rest thought it was just an unruly pitch invasion halting the game for a quarter of an hour. Doctors and countless willing helpers tended those hurt and behind the stand everything that could be improvised for splints and stretchers was feverishly broken by people never before exposed to the ghastly spectacle of the injured and the dying. Hidden from the gaze of the multitude, vehicles of all types loaded with casualties went to and fro from Ibrox to the infirmaries.

The first the players knew of the tragedy was when they went to the dressing rooms at half time and had to step over the bodies of the dead and injured. They had no idea of the heroic rescue work that had gone on while they had been giving their all on the football pitch. Wisely the officials had also kept the knowledge from the spectators, as a stampede might have followed had they known. Most of the players were sickened and many helpers fainted. One was heard to call out 'Is there any brandy about. I feel sick. Don't you see the man's neck is broken.' The officials appealed to the players to keep a tight lip and go out again. Unwillingly, they did, emerging from the pavilion tormented with

The collapsed stand at Ibrox in 1902.

the horror they had left behind, and to their everlasting credit they finished a game that had no further interest for them.

The result of the International (a 1-1 draw) found no place in the records. It was declared 'Unofficial', as was a second International played at Birmingham in aid of the relief fund for the victims. Altogether, 25 people died and over 500 were injured. The English FA donated £4,000 and extended the season by three days to enable clubs to play matches to swell the fund, finally amounting to around £28,000. All 200 police officers on duty at Ibrox on that fateful day donated their earnings.

That the spectators themselves had been responsible for the disaster made it even more terrible. It happened because of their enthusiasm for Bobby Templeton, a Kilmarnock player making his début for Scotland. His fame as a dribbler had preceded him and none matched his skill when taking a corner-kick. All eyes were on him as he gave 'Kelly' Houlker the slip and dribbled towards the corner flag. On tiptoes the spectators in the western terrace were intent on watching the end of the run. The pressure of those behind caused a downward surge, and the sudden extra weight weakened the wooden platform, triggering the disaster.

At the official enquiry no definite conclusion was reached and blame was apportioned to no-one. No claims for compensation could be made against Rangers, the SFA having leased the ground for the game, as the international team had no permanent home at the time.

1909: Riot at Scottish Cup Final Replay — Hampden a Battlefield

The result of the 1909 Scottish Cup Final between Celtic and Rangers was a draw. At Hampden Park on Saturday 17 April, 70,000 fans watched the replay, which also ended in a draw. While the Celtic players disagreed with the referee's decision not to play extra time, Rangers accepted it and left the field, leaving their opponents arguing. A few minutes later Celtic also left the field.

No sooner had the last player entered the pavilion when a hooligan rushed onto the field shouting for others to follow. Within seconds fans were swarming in the direction of the pavilion apparently intent on getting at the players. Fortunately, however, they were thwarted by about 40 constables forming a human chain between them and the pavilion entrance. Having failed to get to the players, the mob turned on the police, hailing them with stones, bricks and bottles. The police withstood the attack, but with the mob increasing and becoming more menacing minute by minute, they drew batons and charged. When several rioters were knocked down, the remainder rushed to the centre of the field, where they fought amongst themselves, uprooted the goalposts and tore the nets to shreds.

When the rioters again tried to get into the pavilion mounted policemen charged, scattering them in all directions, followed by constables on foot. Hampden then became a battlefield, with isolated groups of constables defending themselves from thousands of rampaging fans. An onlooker, a Scot on holiday from Africa, said, 'I have seen the naked savage in a frenzy when defending his home, but never have I seen human beings exhibit fury so fierce, anger so intense, and cowardice so loathsome.' The riot accelerated until parts of the terracing and some of the pay boxes were on fire. When the firemen arrived, as well as being brutally assaulted, their hoses were cut. At that point, witnesses were treated to the astonishing sight of firemen and constables charging and stoning the rioters in an attempt to protect the hoses. It took 300 policemen and dozens of firemen (who turned their hoses on the rioters), until 7p.m., to clear the field. In all, 45 police officers were injured, 14 seriously. Firemen and ambulancemen were also injured, many seriously. Ironically, the rioters got off lightly. Of the 130 treated for injuries, only 30 were hospitalised. Apart from the injuries and damage sustained, the outcome of the day's events was that the SFA retained the Scottish Cup for that year and the players' medals were withheld.

1971: The Ibrox Disaster — Stairway of Death

On 2 January 1971 the country was stunned by a second disaster at Ibrox Stadium — one even more devastating than that of 1902, then the worst in the history of football.

Watched by 80,000 spectators, the traditional New Year match between Rangers and Celtic had been hard and tense and appeared to be heading for a goalless draw, that is, until the 89th minute, when a Bobby Lennox shot struck the crossbar and on the rebound was headed into the net by Jimmy Johnstone. The goal seemed certain to give Celtic its first New Year victory at Ibrox since 1921, but when Rangers swept forward in one last attack Colin Stein hammered home an equaliser.

When the final whistle sounded the fans turned to leave the stadium, those at the Copeland Road end in jubilation at Rangers' late equaliser, which is when the disaster happened. On Stairway 13, leading from the then Copland Road terracing, the crowd descended the steep exit almost as one body, with no-one having control of their individual movements. Not being able to cope with the tremendous surge of downward pressure, the staircase's steel barriers gave way and within seconds people were dead. Minutes later bodies were piled six feet deep on the stair and one report described how the crowd had just caved in like a pack of cards as if all of them were falling into a huge hole.

Immense force had buckled and twisted the central steel barriers running up the steps vertically like thin spines, and there was no escape from the stairway of death except for those close enough and able enough to climb over the outer wooden barriers which had held solidly. Sixty-six Rangers' supporters died; 145 were injured. The official cause of death was 'traumatic asphyxiation' (suffocation). Of the dead, 32 were teenagers, five of them Rangers' supporters, aged between 12 and 15, who had travelled from Fife to see the game.

Amazingly most of the crowd went home unaware of the accident. The Rangers boardroom was in total disarray — unable, or unwilling, to grasp the enormity of what had happened. It was manager, Willie Waddell, who took control, acting as spokesman for the Club, organising representation at funerals and hospital visits. Sombre faced Rangers players, obviously still numbed by the tragedy, visited the injured in hospital. Wearing black ties, they stood at bedsides listening avidly to the survivors' graphic accounts of what happened to them.

One of the saddest stories was that of 14-year-old Jim Miller. He told the players:

> I'll never forget it. I was with my two big pals, one is 19 and the other was 36. We usually hug each other to keep together when we are leaving the ground, but this time we got separated at the top of the stairs. I saw the oldest one, Robert McAdam, being swept away…he's dead now. In the crush a man was holding me. He kept saying, 'keep up son', over and over and then one of the metal barriers gave and we crashed through it. People were falling on top of us. I was scared stiff. There was bodies, arms and legs sticking out everywhere. I didn't realise that many of them were already dead.

He then added quietly: 'Robert is dead now…he used to look after me at the game.' As the Rangers players walked down the ward chatting quietly to the patients, one of them, Colin Stein, shook his head sadly saying, 'Terrible…terrible.'

Players and officials of both clubs stood together at funeral services as they did at the memorial service at Glasgow Cathedral and at a requiem mass at St Andrew's Roman Catholic Cathedral. The Lord Provost's Disaster Fund was set up to help families of the bereaved, with both clubs making substantial contributions.

Newspapers immediately claimed that the disaster had been caused by departing Rangers fans who, on hearing the roar which greeted Stein's goal, turned back to run up Stairway 13 to the terracing, colliding with those coming down. Later, however, this theory was strongly disputed, with witnesses stressing that the crowd had stayed on to the very end and was heading in the same direction when tragedy struck. As to what really happened, I suppose no-one will ever really know, but witnesses suggested that it could have been caused by someone falling over two boys bending down to pick up items thrown in the air in celebration of the late equaliser, or by the fan seen toppling from another's shoulders near the top of Stairway 13. Most supported the latter explanation.

Sheriff Irvine Smith presided over the official enquiry which severely criticised Rangers' directors. The tragedy had been waiting to happen. There had been warnings — three previous accidents on the same stairway in the 1960s. Two dead and 44 injured in 1961, 11 hurt in 1967 and 30 in 1969. The club had been reluctant to take expert advice on ground safety, although £150,000 had been spent on improvements over the previous decade. Directors' and staff's evidence was confused and contradictory, and incredibly, there was only a vague recollection of a visit some months earlier by Chief Inspector Nicholson to inspect the stairway, and no-one had a clue as to who had accompanied the police round the stadium on that occasion. At the end of the 14-day inquiry, Sheriff Smith concluded, 'Rarely can an organisation of the size and significance of Rangers Football Club have succeeded in conducting their business with records so sparse, so carelessly kept, so inaccurately written and so indifferently stored.' Astonishingly, although the findings of the inquiry severely criticised Rangers on safety matters, it exonerated the club, or individual officials, from blame. At the time of the tragedy there were no established guidelines for clubs to follow. Police and local authorities were powerless to impose conditions or to order clubs to improve the safety of their grounds, and it was not until 1975, with the passing of the Safety of Sports Ground Act, that things began to change, although subsequent disasters at Bradford in 1985 and Hillsborough in 1989 showed that lessons still had to be learned.

Before the Old Firm game at Ibrox on 2 January 1991, David Murray, Chairman of Rangers Football Club, unveiled a plaque commemorating the 20th anniversary of the 1971 disaster. However, the most fitting tribute to the memory of the 66 Rangers fans who died was the reconstruction of Ibrox Stadium, and let's hope that with today's all-seated stadia such disasters will never happen again, and that spectators can relax and concentrate on the game without worrying about their safety.

'SO YOU KNOW GLASGOW?'
A HUNDRED QUESTIONS

1. Where was St Mungo born?

2. To which hospital was the first woman gynaecologist in Glasgow appointed in 1905?

3. Which aqueduct in Glasgow was built over 200 years ago?

4. How did Schipka Pass, the short passage which leads from Gallowgate to London Road, get its name?

5. Why were herring nicknamed 'Glasgow Magistrates'?

6. When was Black Saturday and why was it so called?

7. Were garnets ever found in Garnethill?

8. Which Glasgow Church was nicknamed 'The Whistling Kirk'?

9. Where did the name St Enoch come from?

10. From which ancient building did the Town Council allow stones to be removed for the building of The Saracen's Head Inn?

11. Which city church's bell has the following inscription: 'I to the Church the people call and to the grave I summon all?'

12. How did Trongate get its name?

13. What was a Wappenschaw?

14. Who said that Glasgow was a beautiful city and the Athens of the north?

15. Where was the first 'Lightning Conductor' installed in Glasgow and who supervised its installation?

16. When was 'Children's Day'?

17. Why was 'The McLennan Arch' erected on Glasgow Green?

18. Which Glasgow Bridge cost £6.5 million to build?

19. What is the oldest house in Glasgow, and where is it?

20. What is the name of Glasgow's oldest restaurant?

21. When was the Concert Hall in Buchanan Street opened?

22. Where can the only statue of William Shakespeare in Glasgow be seen?

23. What was the first building to be opened exclusively for the showing of films called?

24. How did Bath Street get its name?

25. Which bridge across the Clyde was originally known as the halfpenny bridge?

26. How did Paddy's Market in the Briggait get its name?

27. Which world-famous detective was born in the Gorbals in 1819?

28. Which Lord Provost of Glasgow earned himself the nickname Lazarus?

29. Which Glasgow-born actress who staged over 100 plays in her own theatre in Rutherglen gave a start to the careers of actors such as Gordon Jackson and Nicholas Parsons, who went on to fame in films and on TV?

30. How did the Broomielaw get its name?

31. Who invented the 'Mackintosh' raincoat?

32. Which company built the R34, the first airship to cross the Atlantic?

33. What is unique about the Pavilion Theatre in Hope Street?

34. Where was the first tearoom in the world opened and by who?

35. Where in Glasgow did A.G. Barr PLC, famous for Scotland's other national drink, Irn Bru, start its business?

36. Who was Scotland's first World Boxing Champion?

37. What was the name of the famous burn which used to flow past the Cathedral?

38. Where was the venue of the first International Football Match between Scotland and England in 1872?

39. Which painting, when it was bought in 1952 for £8,200 by Tom Honeyman, the director of the Kelvingrove Art Gallery, was the subject of much criticism?

40. Where in Scotland would you find the largest collection of books by, and about Robert Burns in the world?

41. How did the 'Hielandman's Umbrella', the Central Station viaduct, get its name?

42. When Glasgow-born actor Duncan MacRae's name is mentioned, it is usually because of his memorable renderings of the 'Wee Cock Sparra', but what were some of the films in which this fine actor played important roles?

43. What Glasgow newspaper is the oldest still in publication in Scotland?

44. In which year did Hampden Park, Queen's Park home ground, open?

45. What is the oldest public park in Europe, dating back over 800 years?

46. Where is William Miller, the author of the poem 'Wee Willie Winkie' buried?

47. What now stands on the site of Queen's Dock, Stobcross, which was infilled in 1969?

48. Who performed the world's first antiseptic surgery in Glasgow Royal Infirmary in 1865?

49. What is Cleopatra's Needle on Glasgow Green?

50. What statue sits outside the Gallery of Modern Art in Queen Street?

51. Which building, apart from Glasgow Cathedral, is the oldest still used for its original purpose?

52. What is Glasgow's answer to the Leaning Tower of Pisa?

53. Which was the first Boy Scout troop?

54. Where was Glasgow University sited before it moved to Gilmorehill in 1870?

55. Which youth movement was founded in Glasgow in 1883? .

56. How did Sauchiehall Street get its name?

57. What was the Glasgow Film Theatre originally called?

58. How long is the River Clyde?

59. What village was demolished to make way for the Central Station, opened in 1879?

60. In what well-known building in Robertson Street (not connected with the law) are there prison cells?

61. What was the name of Glasgow's first bank?

62. What does the name Ibrox mean?

63. When were Glasgow's City Chambers built?

64. When did the last tramcar run on Glasgow's streets?

65. Who was Rab Ha?

66. What special provision was made for courting couples at Green's Playhouse, the 4,000-seater cinema that once stood at the corner of Renfield/Renfrew Streets?

67. Which building started life as a Tobacco Lord's mansion and is now an art gallery?

68. Where was the original home of the Glasgow Transport Museum, which is now housed in the Kelvin Hall?

69. Which act featured at the final week in 1963 of the Glasgow Empire Theatre?

70. Hampden Park is Scotland's national football stadium and Queen's Park FC's home ground. Were did Queen's Park play when the club was formed in 1867?

71. In what inn did Robert Burns lodge when he visited Glasgow in 1787 and 1788?

72. What had grocer Thomas Lipton, Detective Alan Pinkerton and boxer Benny Lynch have in common?

73. What rhyme describes the emblems on Glasgow's coat-of-arms?

74. What is unique about the statue of King Billy in Cathedral Square?

75. Where was James Watt walking in 1765 when he hit on the idea of a separate condenser that was to lead to his name becoming synonymous with the emergence of the steam engine?

76. True or false? The main entrance to the Kelvingrove Art Gallery and Museum is in Sauchiehall Street.

77. Which is Glasgow's oldest surviving station?

78. The Trades House was formed in the 16th century to represent 14 incorporated trades in the city. Name six of these?

79. Which building in Glasgow faces the Ka'aba (House of God) in Mecca?

80. Which Glasgow infirmary was opened in 1794?

81. Which great Scottish character actor is remembered among other things for his rendering of 'I Belong to Glasgow'?

82. True of false — Celtic is the senior member of the old firm?

83. Name a Glasgow street called after a famous military leader?

84. True or false? Sir William Burrell who gifted his magnificent collection of masterpieces and collectors' items to Glasgow, was at one time a Glasgow councillor and housing convener.

85. Which Scottish actor who was educated at Finnieston School is fondly remembered for the role of the skipper of the Clyde puffer, the Vital Spark in the Para Handy TV series?

86. Who was the first man to be commemorated by a statue in George Square?

87. Name four Glasgow landmarks situated in Glasgow Green?

88. Was comedian Will Fyffe, famous for his renderings of I' Belong to Glasgow', actually a native of the city?

89. Whose motto, 'work hard an' keep the heid', made her a millionaire?

90. What was the former name of the Glasgow Citizens Theatre in the Gorbals?

91. What was the former Templeton's Carpet Factory in Glasgow Green built to resemble?

92. True or False? *Maid of the Loch*, which was built at the yard of Anthony and John Inglis at Pointhouse-on-Clyde, was the last paddle-steamer to be built in Britain.

93. Who were the Beehives, the Parlour Boys, the Norman Conks and the Billy Boys?

94. Who were the Lisbon Lions?

95. Whose banana boots would you find in the People's Palace?

96. Johnnie Stark was the anti-hero of which novel about Glasgow life in the 1930s?

97. Where is the Mackintosh house?

98. Which Glasgow market has a connection with Ailsa Craig?

99. Which shipyards comprised Upper Clyde Shipbuilders Ltd., when it was set up in 1966?

100 Name five of the artists who were collectively known as 'The Glasgow Boys'?

A HUNDRED ANSWERS

1. Culross in Fife in AD 518.

2. The Victoria Infirmary.

3. The Kelvin Aqueduct.

4. After a Balkan pass, important in the Russian-Turkish War of 1877.

5. As fish merchants landing herring at the Broomielaw had to send specimens to the River Bailie, naturally the best and largest were picked, therefore fat herring were nicknamed 'Glasgow Magistrates'.

6. On 5 April 1902 part of the terracing at Ibrox Stadium collapsed during an international match between Scotland and England, killing 25 and injuring over 500; 587 people eventually received compensation.

7. No. The district was named after Dr Garnet.

8. St Andrew's Episcopal Church (1750), the first Glasgow church to have an organ, which was Calvinistically referred to as 'A Kist of Whistles' — hence the name.

9. The mother of St Mungo was Thenew and St Enoch is said to be a corruption of Thenew.

10. Stones were taken from the Bishop's Castle by permission of the Town Council as the Castle was in a sad state of repair.

11. The bell is in St George's Church (1809) in Buchanan Street.

12. From the weighing machine or 'tron' erected around 1500 in St Thenaw's Gait which ran from The Cross to the West Port (where Argyle Street now starts).

13. A Wappenschaw was the showing of weapons when men of Glasgow, by law, had to practise archery, which took place at 'The Butts', later the site of the Barracks at the corner of Barrack Street and Gallowgate.

14. Daniel Defoe, in his book of 1727, written after he had toured Scotland.

15. The first lightning conductor in Glasgow was erected on the steeple of the old University in High Street in 1772, under the supervision of American statesman, Benjamin Franklin.

16. Children's Day was instituted in 1887, the year of Queen Victoria's Diamond Jubilee, and was again held on Saturday 27 May 1899. About 89,000 children were entertained in the seven public parks and about 117,000 witnessed this.

17. When the Assembly Rooms in Ingram Street were replaced, the arch, which was part of the façade at first-storey height, was saved, thanks to the generosity of Bailie McLennan, who paid for it to be removed to the Charlotte Street entrance to Glasgow Green. Later it was removed to its present position at the Saltmarket entrance to the Green.

18. Kingston Bridge, opened in 1970.

19. Provand's Lordship in Castle Street, built in 1474 by Bishop Andrew Muirhead.

20. Sloans, in the Argyll Arcade, which originated from a coffee house opened in Morrison's Court in 1797 by businessman John Morrison.

21. 1990.

22. The Citizens Theatre.

23. Pringle's Picture Palace, near Charing Cross in Sauchiehall Street, opened in 1907.

24. It was the site of the first public baths in the city, which William Harley built in 1810 with money made by selling water at a halfpenny a pail.

25. The suspension bridge, opened in 1853. It got its nickname because a halfpenny toll was charged to cross it.

26. In the 1840s it was where famine-stricken Irish immigrants sold their clothes to feed their families.

27. Alan Pinkerton, who founded the Pinkerton Detective Agency in America.

28. Pat Lally, because every time it seemed sure his political career in Glasgow was dead, it was resurrected.

29. Molly Urquhart, who died in 1977.

30. From broom bushes, which used to grow abundantly of the banks of the Clyde, and from the old Scots word 'law', meaning a grassy slope or meadow. Therefore, Broomielaw means 'a meadow covered with golden broom'.

31. Charles Mackintosh in 1842. He worked in his father's chemical works in Dennistoun.

32. William Beardmore.

33. It has a sliding roof, the intention being to open it on hot nights.

34. At the corner of Queen Street/Argyle Street by Stuart Cranston, a Glasgow tea merchant.

35. Parkhead in 1904.

36. Flyweight Benny Lynch, born in Florence Street, Gorbals. Benny died at the age of 33, drunken and destitute.

37. The Molendinar, which was covered in years ago and is now a sewer.

38. The West of Scotland Cricket Ground in Partick. The score was a goal-less draw and all the players in the Scottish team were from Queens Park Football Club, Glasgow's oldest club having been founded in 1867.

39. Salvador Dali's *Christ of St John of the Cross*. It was thought scandalous to pay so much for a picture out of public funds. However, the purchase turned out to be an excellent investment and was transferred to the Museum of Religion which opened in the Cathedral Precinct in 1993.

40. The Mitchell Library in North Street opened in 1911. The library owes its existence to tobacco manufacturer Stephen Mitchell, who left £66,998.10s 6d when he died to start a fund to found it.

41. Because in the days when people left the Highlands and Islands to find work in Glasgow they were told before they left to go on a Sunday afternoon or evening to certain places under the 'Umbrella' where they would find other exiles gathered.

42. *Whisky Galore, Geordie, Tunes of Glory, Greyfriars Bobby*, etc.

43. The Herald, which first appeared in 1783.

44. In 1913.

45. Glasgow Green.

46. In the old Kirkyard in Tollcross. However, there is a memorial to him in the Necropolis.

47. The Scottish Exhibition and Conference Centre which opened in 1985. Previously the Kelvin Hall had played host to most of the events.

48. Joseph Lister.

49. It is not only the first monument to be erected in the city but the first in Britain to be erected in honour of Admiral Lord Nelson. It was built in 1806 by architect David Hamilton, 15 years before London's monument in Trafalgar Square.

50. The finest in Glasgow, that of The Duke of Wellington on horseback sculpted by Baron Marochetti in the 1820s. The public's habit of adorning the Duke's head with a traffic cone is a bone of contention with the Council, as it thinks it demeaning. However, the Council appears to be losing the battle, as no sooner is the cone removed than another replaces it.

51. The Trade's House in Glassford Street, designed by Robert Adam and completed in 1794. The 14 incorporated Trades of Glasgow still meet there.

52. The Cameron Fountain at Charing Cross which, because of the traffic thundering past, leans drunkenly to the right. It was made by Doulton in 1896 and commemorates Sir Charles Cameron in recognition of his services to Glasgow during his first 21 years in Parliament.

53. The 1st Glasgow Boy Scout Troop, registered in 1908.

54. High Street.

55. The Boys' Brigade by William Smith, its objective being 'The advancement of God's Kingdom among boys and the promotion of habits of reverence, discipline, self-respect, and all that tends towards a true Christian manliness'.

56. Sauchiehall Street was formed on a 'haugh' or meadow where 'saugh' or willow trees grew. It is a corruption of Sauchiehaugh.

57. The Cosmo, built in 1939 by George Singleton (Mr Cosmo) to cater for continental and universal films of the time.

58. 106 miles, the 3rd longest river in Scotland behind the Tay and Spey respectively.

59. Grahamstown, at the time considered to be on the outskirts of the city. It had only one street, Alston Street, which ran diagonally from what is now the corner of Hope Street to the corner of Union Street.

60. The magnificent Clyde Port building which once served as a marine jail, the cells being in the basement.

61. The Shipbank, which opened in 1750 at the corner of Saltmarket and Bridgegate, where the Shipbank pub now stands.

62. The place of the badger, with 'brock' being the old Scots word for badger.

63. 1883, by London-based Paisley-born architect William Young. Over 10 million bricks were used, which were then fronted with stone to give the appearance of a stone building.

64. 4 September 1962, when a quarter of a million people turned out to wave goodbye to it.

65. The 'Glesca Glutton', properly known as Robert Hall. He used to take bets that he could out-eat anyone, and once ate a whole calf at one go.

66. Couples could opt for the golden divans in the balcony, cosy, private seats which provided a measure of privacy while still allowing a view of the screen.

67. The former Cunninghame Mansion built by William Cunninghame around 1750, now part of The Gallery of Modern Art in Queen Street.

68. The old tram repair depot in Albert Road.

69. The Red Army Ensemble.

70. Queen's Park recreation ground.

71. The Black Bull Inn, the site now occupied by Marks & Spencer's store.

72. They were all born in the Gorbals.

73. This is the bird that never flew
    This is the tree that never grew
    This is the fish that never swam
    This is the bell that never rang.

74. Its tail moves when the wind blows because its attached by a ball-and-socket arrangement.

75. In Glasgow Green, which in Watt's day was used as a place for washing and drying clothes.

76. False. The main entrance is the one inside the park facing north across the Kelvin Valley.

77. Queen Street, which opened in 1842.

78. Masons, Wrights, Coopers, Fleshers, Hammermen, Tailors, Bakers, Cordiners, Maltmen, Weavers, Skinners, Barbers, Dyers, Gardeners.

79. The Central Mosque and Islamic Centre at Gorbals Cross, built between 1979 and 1984 at a cost of £3,000,000.

80. The Royal Infirmary, regarded from the word go as a leading medical school, and to this day one of Scotland's finest centres for medical education.

81. Will Fyffe.

82. False. Rangers FC was founded in 1873; Celtic not until 1888.

83. Wellington Street.

84. True.

85. Roddy McMillan.

86. Sir John Moore, who was educated at Glasgow High School. He joined the army at 15 and had a distinguished military career which culminated in his death at Corunna. There, according to Napoleon, 'his talents and firmness alone saved the British Army from destruction'. He was referred to as 'the hero of Corunna'.

87. The People's Palace (the museum of Glasgow's social and industrial history), the Doulton Fountain, the Nelson Monument and the McLennan Arch.

88. No, he was born in Dundee.

89. Maggie McIver.

90. The Princess Theatre which opened in 1878 as Her Majesty's Theatre.

91. The Doge's Palace in Venice, replicated in coloured brick by architect William Leiper.

92. True.

93. Glasgow gangs of the 20s and 30s.

94. The Celtic players who beat Inter Milan in the final of the European Cup in Lisbon in 1967.

95. Billy Connolly's.

96. *No Mean City*, by Alexander McArthur and H. Kingsley Long.

97. It is part of the Hunterian Art Gallery. It reconstructs the main rooms of the Glasgow home of architect Charles Rennie Mackintosh.

98. Paddy's Market, Paddy's Milestone being another name for Ailsa Craig.

99. John Brown's, Connell's, Fairfield's and Stephen's, with Yarrow as an associate.

100. E.A. Hornel, D.Y. Cameron, John Lavery, William Kennedy, James Guthrie, Stuart Park, James Paterson, George Henry and E.A. Walton.